Ally!

You are lovely inside
& out. It was an
Honor to meet you!
Follow Your Dreams!

Making
Relationships
Matter

Author David D. Coleman
has won 9
National Speakers Association Awards

1996, 2001, 2002
from the National Association for Campus Activities (NACA)

1996, 1997, 2000, 2001, 2002, 2003
from Campus Activities Magazine

Making
Relationships
Matter

Nine Ways to Stay in Love for Life

By David D. Coleman
The Dating Doctor

Edited by:
Claudia Cornette
Darline Clemens

Making Relationships Matter

Text copyright © 2003 by David D. Coleman

First U.S. edition 2003
Printed in China
Coleman, David D., 1961-
    Making relationships matter: nine ways to stay
in love for life / by David D. Coleman.
        p.cm.
        ISBN 0-9717843-2-9

    1.Love. 2. Intimacy (Psychology) 3. Man-
woman relationships. I. Title.

        BF575.L8C65 2003   158.2
                QB133-1294

9504 Bainbrook
Cincinnati, Ohio 45249
www.angelbea.com

Dedication

This book is dedicated to my daughters, Shannon and Natalie. I hope you will use this book as a guide to find the lifelong love you deserve. Thank you both for bringing more joy and love to my life than I could ever express in words.

Special Thanks:

To my wife, Diane, for allowing me the time it took to write this book.

To Kat and Ash Shehata for believing in me.

To Claudia Cornett for your tough love and guidance.

To Darline Clemens because there would be no book if you had not gone the extra mile for me and this project.

To Jo McElwee for your work on the cover and jacket.

To Anne Bakker for your thoughtful management of my career and never-ending words of encouragement.

To Dr. Will Keim for making me sit down and start this project for real.

To Curtis Zimmerman for changing my life and for teaching me that goals really do matter.

Contents

Foreword

David Coleman is a person you can trust. I have observed him in front of two thousand people, I have seen him comfort a person one-to-one, and I have been blessed to sit and break bread with his family and wonder at the relationship he has with his daughters and his wife. *Making Relationships Matter* will heal broken relationships. It will empower new relationships to be better. It will finally allow the readers to let go of things that happened in the past and free the individual to start again. From early stories about his father that will move you to tears to contemporary gems such as, "Our children are our legacy to people we will never meet," David Coleman understands human relationships and how to make them better. I have often thought that the only difference between David and most of the so-called "relationship experts" you see on television is that David knows what he is talking about and can actually live out his teachings in his daily life.

After twenty years on the road and presentations to over two million people from all walks of life, I can easily tell you who is "the wheat" and who is "the chaff." David Coleman is a harvest of sound advice based on ethical conduct resulting in a man who talks the talk and walks the walk.

The most important aspect of my life is my role as a father. I would lie down and give up my heart for one of my four wonderful children. I would trust each of them to David's care and have made sure that they have been present at his presentations and had access to his teachings. I can say to you without reservation that my children, myself, and anyone who hears or reads his message will be a better person for it. It is not often that a parent's credibility goes up when his or her children sit and listen to a friend speak on the importance of caring, of loving, of making relationships matter. My children say to me, "You know him?" "Yes." "That's really cool, Dad. He's great." I would trust my children to his care: Is there higher praise than this?

David Coleman, the Dating Doctor, as he is known internationally, is the real deal. Read his book. Listen to his compact disc. Watch his videos. Become the person you have always dreamed you could become. I know I am better for having met him and you too will soon agree that he has a gift for helping each of us achieve the ability to actualize our full potential in the relationships that shape and drive our lives. His insights are right on target, his understandings wise, and his sincere care for you as a person undeniable. Thank God for someone who knows the secret to life-giving relationships. And thank God for someone who will share this knowledge with the rest of us. That someone is David Coleman!

Will Keim, Ph.D., Intercollegiate Chaplain Educator and Author, *The Education of Character; Spirit Journey; Life After College; The Truth About College; The Tao Of Christ; Wit & Wisdom; Chicken Soup For The College Soul*

Introduction

In all honesty, I did not start out to become "The Dating Doctor" or a "relationship expert." In fact, as a child I envisioned myself becoming a veterinarian. High school chemistry immediately brought me to the realization that the medical arts were not going to play a prominent role in my future. But during my sophomore year in college I became aware that I had been blessed with the gift of discernment. I seemed to have an ability to introduce people who needed to meet one another. I was told time and again that I possessed a gift for connecting with new acquaintances on a deep level, and quickly gauging personal situations. By listening to and hearing the stories that people needed to share, I found myself offering ideas and solutions to various forms of faltering relationships.

Over the following decades, the more I worked with people on their relationships, the more I learned. I learned what situations people faced most often and found most difficult, such as meeting others, effectively communicating, ending dead-end relationships, or keeping the passion alive in a long-term relationship. The advice I offered was appreciated and respected and I grew to be a trusted resource for many people.

I have been repeatedly asked when I was going to author a book with my thoughts, suggestions, and theories on love, dating, relationships, and marriage. My standard answer was always, "Not yet. It just isn't the right time." Well, the time is now right not only for me, but also for others as the reality in relationships is that they require understanding of self and others.

I wrote this book because I would like to make an impact on your life. You may be lonely and in pain. You may feel that you are unlovable, jinxed, or "damaged goods." You may feel unsure of where to begin or lack the bravery to do so and you need a jumpstart. You may feel that you don't matter and that there is no one out there who is right for you. Or, you may be stuck in a loveless relationship or stagnant marriage that yields little hope. You do matter, your relationships matter, your life matters, and there is hope. Many people lack the courage to try something new, to attempt to live beyond their comfort level or solve their own problems. They lack the knowledge of how to make change happen and the daring to begin. This book will encourage you and give you knowledge. It will instill in you the desire to use that knowledge and take the action needed for you to be successful and satisfied.

The events of September 11, 2001, reminded

many of us that life and relationships are fragile. There is no time to waste. Time is precious and we never get a wasted day back. If you are willing to move ahead with examining your relationships and making positive changes in your life, then this book was written for you.

I stress the urgency in not wasting your time in unfitting relationships. Relationships take time to develop and perhaps you find yourself in relationships that seem to repeat themselves. My speaking engagements and radio and television appearances have allowed me to interact with hundreds of thousands of people. Their questions and stories and comments reveal relationship histories that break down into five identifiable categories. These categories are:

1. **Never been kissed.** These individuals rarely date and are concerned that this pattern will follow them throughout their lives causing them to feel vulnerable and lonely. Many seem to have the **Uns**—meaning they believe that they are **un**lovable, **un**wanted, **un**skilled, **un**attractive, and are attracted to people who are **un**available to them. This makes them feel considerably **un**comfortable, **un**desirable, and **un**happy.

2. **Been kissed too often, by too many, for too long.** These people are social butterflies and

have "been there and done that" when it comes to dating, marriage, divorce, and relationships. Very little surprises them and they have become jaded by the entire process. It is easier for them to laugh off their relationship failures than to admit they are not being successful. They have given so many pieces of their hearts, minds, bodies, and souls to others that they have little left to commit to the right person if and when that person comes along.

3. **Everyone's best friend, but no one's lover.** These are the nice guys and sweet gals who are well-known and apparently liked by many but can't translate their popularity into success in the social dating arena. Their low self-confidence and poor self-esteem are hurting their chances of relationship success, and they are at a loss to figure out why everyone wants to be around them but no one truly wants to be *with* them.

4. **Marathoners.** These people have been involved in long-term relationships and/or marriages where the fire has long since burned out. They feel trapped in relationships in which they remain out of obligation. Some want their relationships to end but don't know how to make it happen, while others aren't sure they are ready to terminate what they have for fear that they might not find someone else with whom to share their lives. For many,

being unhappy is preferable to being alone.

5. **Nomads.** These people are not dating, not in a relationship, not sure why, not sure where they are headed, and not sure it will change. They yearn for a compass that leads them anywhere but to a mirage of what *could be and should be* for them socially.

My advice to the members of all five groups is to identify the pattern and find out how and why it has developed. It is important to answer these questions so that you can learn to be yourself. To be yourself you need to accept and celebrate your uniqueness. You need to act in a way that is consistent with your values and let others react as they need to in relation to you. You need to know your strengths, weaknesses, and idiosyncrasies and use them as you search for the love you deserve and desire. No one said this would be easy, but these are the important first steps to building hope and confidence and enacting change. You need to believe in yourself before you can expect others to believe in you.

My goal is to help readers find out how to BE the type of person who makes his or her personal relationships matter. Anecdotes, stories, and examples will help you to understand and use important relationship principles on a daily basis. My hope is you will become more courageous, cognizant of your value, respectful, forgiving, passionate, committed, spiritual, trustworthy, healthy, and ultimately actively involved in your relationships.

In the movie *The Shawshank Redemption*, Andy Dufresne is sitting in the prison yard talking with his closest friend, Ellis Boyd "Red" Redding. They are discussing whether having hope for the future while being inmates in prison is positive or harmful. Andy considers his life and future and then makes a decision. "It is either time to get busy living or get busy dying," he says. He chooses to get busy living.

You may feel as if you are dying a little inside every day because of chronic relationship failure or a romantic void in your life. You begin to doubt yourself more each day. I want this book to be your lifeline and enable you to get busy living, today. The major limitations you face in life are those you place in front of yourself and it is time for those barriers to begin to disappear today. Excuses need to be replaced by action. Self-pity needs to be replaced by self-interest and selfless love. Today you become your biggest fan and toughest critic, but with the road map you hold in your hands, your future destination to relationships that matter is clearly in sight.

"A BRAVE MAN IS NO DIFFERENT
THAN AN ORDINARY MAN,
HE IS JUST BRAVER FOR FIVE
MINUTES LONGER."

— RALPH WALDO EMERSON

CHAPTER 1

Be Courageous

Relationships take courage. Sometimes they take a little and sometimes they take quite a bit more. It was July 4, 1966. I was six years old and on summer vacation with my parents and two teenage sisters. I woke up to the rising sun and looked out the window of my cabin. I just couldn't sleep any longer because today my father was taking me fishing for the first time. Just me. Dad had primed me all week that we would catch "The Big One," and I was ready.

The setting was Port Clinton, a small town near Lake Erie in northern Ohio, and a fishing paradise. My father and I had previously scoped out the area and found an ideal fishing spot. It was an old bridge in the countryside, just far enough away from the activity of the vacationers nearby, but close enough to sneak back to our cabin if we got bored, tired, in need of a restroom, or any combination thereof. The bridge was three car lengths long and so narrow that only one car could pass at a time, but the guardrail was the perfect height for me to lean against for both comfort and protection.

Dad parked the car safely on the side of the road about half a mile from the bridge and we unloaded our gear and began to walk, talk, and laugh. We were both dressed for battle. My father was in his favorite tan windbreaker and I wore my orange life vest and green army helmet (complete with an adjustable strap under the chin). It was now 7:30 a.m. and I couldn't wait to get my pole in the water. I tugged at my father's coat. "Dad, are we ready yet? I can't catch The Big One until my pole is in the water." Dad smiled patiently, chuckled, and rolled his eyes.

We placed our poles in the water and time passed quickly. Hunger soon overtook us and we nibbled on our sandwiches as we waited for nibbles on our poles. I glanced at my father's watch and saw that it was 10:00. Several hours had vanished in mere minutes. I remember feeling like a human sponge as I absorbed the sights and sounds and presence of my father— in my eyes, the greatest fisherman that ever lived. The sun was bright orange and warmed my face.

The sky was pure aqua and a breath of cool wind whispered through the trees. It was beautiful, peaceful, calm, and perfect. I could have lived in that moment forever.

A low rumble in the distance broke the silence and began to gain on us. The noise got closer and louder until around the corner roared a gang of men on the loudest motorcycles that I have ever heard in my life. They were dressed in combinations of black and brown leather and were swerving and yelling and laughing and cussing, as their long hair and unkempt beards whipped wildly in the wind. My father held me close. As they passed by us, they gunned their engines, raised their voices, cursed, swerved in our direction, and took swipes at us. Within seconds they disappeared around the bend and the growl of the engines faded.

My heart was racing and the contents of my stomach were now collected deep in my throat. There was no bathroom in sight, but I desperately needed one. I was ready to leave and go back to our cabin even if it meant catching no fish, but I didn't want my father to know that I was scared and I didn't want him to be disappointed in me.

He must have sensed that we had not seen the last of the gang for he hastily took my hand and said, "Follow me, son." With no time to make it back to our car, we quickly walked along the bridge until it ended. There was a part in the tall weeds that allowed us to descend down to the water below. Dad held my hand tightly and led me to an area under the bridge where a mixture of gravel and large stones were piled to keep the embankment from eroding. He whispered, "Davey, sit here, don't move, and be very, very quiet. I will come back down and get you as soon as I can. I love you."

My father had barely made it back onto the bridge and picked up his pole when the bikers returned. Although I couldn't see what happened next, the sounds developed into snapshots that have remained in my mind and heart forever. The bikers either forgot that I existed or didn't care, but they proceeded to pummel my father unmercifully. Dad was a peaceful man who had a smile and a sandwich for everyone. I doubt that he even lifted a finger in retaliation, as he was tremendously outnumbered. I remember hearing the bikers laugh, kick my father, spit on him, fire up their engines, and speed away.

Cold, shaking, and nauseous, I was concerned for my father but frozen with fear. I cried, but nothing came out, and I had trouble breathing. I was worried that there were still gang members above waiting for me to appear so they could beat me up as well. I snapped my head to the side as I heard the rustle of someone walking by. It was my father. He walked to the water's edge without so much as a glance in my direction. Visibly shaken, he removed his coat, doused it with water, and used it to clean the blood off his face and hands. He then walked over, forced a smile, took my hand, and said, "Davey, come with me." We walked all the way back to our car where he opened the trunk and placed his stained coat inside. I figured that we were leaving and hoped that we were. I was never going fishing again.

But that is not the decision a courageous person makes. Dad walked me back to the bridge, picked up our scattered fishing poles, and said, "Now let's catch The Big One." My father taught me an important lesson about life that day. He taught me that we all view the world from the pictures in our hearts and he didn't want my snapshot of fishing to be one where you fear for your life and avoid it at all costs. He didn't want the terrifying moment on that bridge to become my predominant memory of time spent outdoors with my family. Nature must have sensed that we needed to end our day on a happy note, as over the next several hours we caught a stringer full of fish. Each one, in my mind, was The Big One.

If my father had not walked me back to that bridge, there is no question that I would have never fished again. But because he did, I now fish regularly and each time I do I recall that time on the bridge with my dad. Yes, the bikers come back too but they quickly fade when I think of my day with my father.

This past Mother's Day, my young daughters and I offered my wife a few hours "off" to do whatever she wanted. The three of us then went to our local "fishing hole" just minutes from our home. Within an hour, my daughters teamed up to catch a twenty-pound catfish. Their eyes were as wide as silver dollars and their smiles stretched from ear to ear, as they pulled and tugged the fish to the shore. "No way. Look how huge it is! We did it!" they repeated over and over. It was a picture that I hope lives in their hearts forever. I've never had to battle a gang of bikers for my daughters' honor but because I encourage them and spend time with them and share my love with them, I think they know that I would.

The Lifelong Effect of Courage

Someday, all too soon, my daughters will grow up, get married, and raise families. And there is a good chance they will take their children fishing. That is the marvelous thing about being courageous and touching lives—you end up affecting people you will never meet or know. My father showed courage on the bridge that day, which instilled courage in me that I now pass on to others. My father didn't just change the pictures in my heart, he changed the pictures in the hearts of my family, friends, co-workers, and neighbors because my interactions with them are more genuine and meaningful. He affected the hearts of those who hear me speak or read my words because I now think of how I can be more courageous for them and with them.

To make your relationships matter, it takes courage and heart. Courage begins with facing the unknown. It is advanced by the moral strength to do something even when you are apprehensive and aren't sure what the outcome will be. For example, it takes courage to ask someone out on a date. It is scary to enter into a relationship. It takes discipline of mind and body to remain faithful and positive when there is uncertainty. Courage means that you are willing to run the risk of being hurt and experiencing pain, because the potential of a loving relationship is so wonderful. It takes patience, compromise, and commitment to grow together as one.

Ralph Waldo Emerson once said that "a brave man is no different than an ordinary man, he is just braver for five minutes longer." I encourage you to take five extra minutes, every day, for the rest of your life, to be brave. When an action feels just outside your comfort zone, give it a second look and muster the strength and wherewithal to try. Say hello to a distant friend or family member instead of letting another day pass by. Be the first to say "I'm sorry" or "I love you." Shed a tear when you feel emotional instead of remaining stoic and safe from ridicule. Remember that a life lived in fear is a life half lived.

Capture Every Moment

There is no time to waste. If there is someone to whom you are attracted, let that person know. Smile, make eye contact, and say hello. Be the first to extend your hand and say "Nice to meet you." Pick up the phone and call the person or send a short email, but don't squander another day where you talk yourself out of making the courageous move. If you don't, he or she may meet someone else and never have the opportunity to know you. If you have a thought or feeling to share with someone, say what is on your mind. If you need to apologize to someone, swallow your pride and express your heartfelt regret—and do it today. If you have "feelings" for a "friend" that extend beyond mere friendship, take the risk and let that person know. Tell him or her face-to-face in a non-threatening way—in a way that allows the person to maintain his or her dignity if his or her feelings are not reciprocal. Yes, you may alter a friendship in the process, but the courage to take a risk might gain you a partner and lover for life. If you are proud of someone, applaud his or her effort. If you want to thank someone, convey your gratitude. If you are tired of being lonely, experiment with ways to meet people. Get involved in your church or community. Allow people you trust to arrange for you to meet someone they feel might just be right for you. Place a personal advertisement in a highly respected publication or research and join a reputable match-making service with safeguards for privacy and level of interest. No matter what option you choose, get up, dust yourself off, gather your courage, and begin the process of moving forward.

There are opportunities available on a daily basis that will allow you to be courageous. If you have a story to tell, fire up your keyboard and begin typing or recite into your tape recorder. If you are dissatisfied with an aspect of your life, reflect upon what is causing these feelings and enter into a contract with yourself to make those specific changes. Finally, if you are in conflict with someone, gather and stick to the facts, avoid attacking the person's character, choose an appropriate time, and confront him or her directly, tactfully, appropriately, and honestly. Every day spent in anger is a day stripped of love, respect, and dignity and another day where an issue is left to fester and potentially escalate. Conflict isn't easy to deal with, but it is necessary to reach closure, real closure, if you plan to move forward with your relationships.

To Become More Courageous

So, are you courageous enough to make your relationships matter? Are you prepared to create a new photo album and develop new pictures? Consider this book your personal studio, one where you develop the pictures you want and need to live a life without fear—one where you are the hero and come out on top. Remember though, that to develop vivid pictures, you may need to spend some time in your darkroom alone. You may need time spent in solitude to reflect upon your past experiences, to acknowledge your strengths and weaknesses and to decide what type of person you truly want to be. Courage, change, and happiness all begin from within.

To begin the process of becoming more

courageous, challenge yourself. Face your fears and endure. Attempt new activities. Ride a roller coaster with a friend and take on your fear of heights. Laugh when it is over and feel good about yourself. If you fear the water, take swimming lessons. Work to bring mature closure to a relationship that remains confrontational and uncomfortable. Have the confidence to say hello to someone you have convinced yourself is "out of your league." Declare your dreams, admit your desires, and state your intentions because when you say them out loud, you have something to shoot for. Document your limitations and claim them, then do your best to eliminate them. If you don't do this, you begin to believe that your past will always be your present and thus reduce and diminish your interactions with others. You will continue to limit your experiences and living this way becomes acceptable to you. You begin to settle and accept mediocrity, which is unacceptable. Your lifeless black-and-white photos need to be replaced by new ones in vivid color, and the transformation begins today.

If you have a problem relationship, want to strengthen a current one, or wish to start a new one, you can show courage by:

Being the one who breaks the ice. Make eye contact, smile, and say hello to someone who interests you. Isn't it funny how people seldom remember who broke the ice, but they sure are happy to be standing in a puddle?

Being the first person to bring up important topics or issues that need to be addressed, especially when obvious or subtle tension exists.

Admitting to and claiming your shortcomings and graciously acknowledging your gifts and talents. Ask your love interest to do the same because you truly want to know more about him or her to become closer and more intimate.

Controlling your desire for physical intimacy when it is inappropriate, unwanted, would harm a relationship, and/or place the other person in an uncomfortable or compromising situation. But, when appropriate, let your passion equate to your true feelings for the person.

Appropriately closing all relationships that remain active in some way that are inhibiting you from moving forward toward a more meaningful and satisfying lifestyle.

My father passed away a few years back;

thus, you will never have the chance to meet him, benefit from his grace, experience his sense of humor, or be offered a sandwich (as he felt it was his personal mission to feed everyone he met). But his voice lives on through me as well as through those he loved, so it is with each of us. Every life we touch and every spirit we impact is a direct result of the love and strength others have invested in us. My father taught me by example to be courageous and to strive to create positive and lasting memories for my family and friends. For that I am eternally grateful. My goal now is to create similar memories and feelings for you, so that you can begin to do the same for others.

As you rise from bed each morning keep the words of inspirational speaker and my close friend Curtis Zimmerman in mind: "There is no guarantee that your personal September 11th won't be tomorrow. No one knows when his or her personal September 11th is going to be, but everyone is going to have one. You need to live today to the fullest and treat it as if it were your last because one day you will be right. Remember, there wasn't one person on any of the planes that day who called their stock broker."

He's right and time is wasting.

15

A MAN WHO KNOWS THE PRICE OF EVERYTHING,
KNOWS THE VALUE OF NOTHING.

— Oscar Wilde

CHAPTER 2

Be Valuable

There is a story that takes place in an old Indian village where a young boy named Elon lived with his grandfather. A week before his thirteenth birthday, Elon (which means Godly Tree) asked his grandfather, "Am I a man, Grandfather?" His grandfather replied, "Not quite yet, Elon. The age of thirteen years marks an important date for you, but in order to be considered a man in this tribe, you must kill a deer with only nature to assist you. Then, you must bring the deer back to the village. The tribe will cheer you because they will know that you value and care for them."

So, Elon began his quest. He ventured out into the wilderness taking no tools. He had not traveled far before he spotted a herd of deer. He watched the herd for several days and noticed three things. First, each morning the deer grazed in several places, yet they crossed the same path at about the same time every day to return to the forest. Second, there were two injured deer that lagged behind and were much slower than the others. Third, an old oak tree that stretched across the path had a high branch that was an ideal perch for a surprise attack. Elon was enjoying his time alone with nature. He relished the quiet, the beauty of the wilderness, and the activity of the animals.

During the next few days Elon found a straight and sturdy branch and using a sharp rock he whittled it down, smoothing the sides until it formed a razor-sharp spear. Finally, the day of his thirteenth birthday arrived. He arose just before the sun and headed out to the tree to await the deer. When he arrived, Elon practiced leaping from the branch while driving the stake down with great force into the ground. This was his strategy to kill the deer and become a man.

Elon made sure he was downwind from the herd and squatted upon the branch. He quieted his body and emotions and froze in position. The herd of deer began to cross the path at their regular spot and return to the woods. As he expected, the injured deer were bringing up the rear. When the last deer was directly below him, Elon jumped from the branch, emoting a warrior-like yell, and drove the spear down through the back of the animal. The deer shrieked and began to writhe as the spear pinned it to the ground. Immediately Elon realized that he had missed the heart and lungs. He had not killed the deer. So he reached down and with his bare hands strangled the deer until it gave a final breath. Elon saw the deer's eyes become fixed and felt its head go limp in his hands.

Learning to Assess Value

Elon sobbed as he flung the dead deer over his shoulder and stumbled back to the village. When he arrived home he dropped the deer and began to shout, "Grandfather, where are you, come out here right now and face me. Come out here right now!" His grandfather and the other tribesmen heard Elon's cries and came running. With a sorrowful tone and broken voice, Elon yelled once more at his grandfather, "How could you do this to me? How could you make me kill this deer with my own hands? I don't want to be a man that kills for no purpose."

His grandfather listened to all Elon said. Then he replied, "Elon, you have learned and experienced many things during your wilderness journey, but the love and value of your tribe has returned you home. You did not kill this animal for no purpose. We will use every part of it. Its meat will feed us. The skin will make tents, the fur will clothe the children, the fat will burn to light our way, and the bones will become tools and weapons. You become a man when you appreciate nature for its splendor and beauty and for the important role it plays in the life of our tribe.

Elon bowed his head and apologized. "I am sorry for what I said to you, Grandfather, and for my behavior. I disrespected you. I understand what it means to be a man and I apologize to you all." The deer had provided motivation and importance in the wilderness but was of greater value to the tribe. Elon turned the precious deer over to those for whom it held tremendous value.

On his thirteenth birthday Elon learned about worth and value. Animals, nature, friends, grandparents, manhood, and wisdom — everything is assigned some worth and value. Value is determined by how much you would be affected if someone or something were absent from your life forever. This definition helps us understand how much we value the major aspects of our lives such as our spouse, children, pets, friends, significant other, and our extended family.

Assigning Value

What do people value? People value that which is painful to lose. I appreciate the value of this story. I value my country and our democratic freedoms. I value the changing seasons, music, and the gift of laughter. What would be painful for most people to lose, what would be painful for you to lose? Take out a piece of paper and a writing utensil and take an inventory of what you value. Make a separate list of all of the family, friends, acquaintances, feelings, objects, animals, attributes, activities, types of food, materials, blessings, places, etc., in your life. Now go back and circle only those people or items that would have a major impact on you if they were taken from your life forever. If you could lose something or someone without much disruption to your life, this should not be considered something you value highly. What if I told you that you could circle no more than five options in any given area? This will document what you truly value and what you long to keep as an active part of your life. This exercise can help you make some difficult decisions about what remains a priority in your life when your resources become limited and time is of the essence.

Value Role Models

In the preceding folktale, Elon learned about assessing worth and value from his grandfather. I learned a similar lesson from my mother, Vivian. Mom worked diligently as a registered nurse for twenty-six years, working weekends, holidays, and nights as needed. At the age of fifty-seven, she suffered two severe strokes and several trans ischemic accidents (or mini-strokes). During her illness, she rarely complained. Even when she lost her ability to speak, walk, feed herself, and take care of her most basic needs, she expressed emotion and love through her eyes, smile, and gentle touch. Even though she grimaced in obvious pain, with help she got out of bed every morning and smiled. When she giggled or her eyes widened brightly or narrowed and filled with tears we knew that she was expressing joy, compassion, love, frustration, sorrow, or fear. She delighted in being read to and appeared to be calmed and humbled when we prayed over her. We sensed by her demeanor that she understood that the end of her life here on earth would be but the beginning of her journey.

It was in the condition of ill health that my mother greeted her newborn grandchildren. The first sight of them brought a smile to her face.

The children never saw her walk or heard her talk, yet they eagerly shared with her their latest drawings and report cards and somehow through the wink of an eye, the nod of her head, the raising of a finger, or the faint flash of a smile, she made them feel that they were loved. Many people attended and cried at her funeral. As they paid their last respects, countless individuals spoke of spoke of how their lives were affected by having her in it. She taught many of us about courage and the value of life by fighting for hers every day.

Role models, like my mother was for me, force us to value each moment. Role models are those who face problems, conflict, and adversity with poise, dignity, and grace. Examine the role models in your life and how they engage in relationships with you. People who lack the necessary qualities may engage in relationships in which they begin to take one another for granted, drain the relationship, and lose sight of the value of the relationship. How much is a partner and companion in life worth who loves and is truly loved? The failure to value and make time each day for people and activities that truly matter to us is destructive.

Valuable Questions

How can you measure the value of having people in your life?

Simple: Imagine spending every day of your life completely isolated and void of interactions with others. Imagine having no one to communicate with, no one to share precious or challenging moments with or to compete against. Imagine having no one to love or be loved by physically, emotionally, intellectually, and spiritually. Imagine the loneliness associated with working by yourself, and then coming home and having no one to recount the day's successes and failures with. People are valuable.

How can you measure your own true worth and value?

Take a lead from Jimmy Stewart in the movie *It's a Wonderful Life,* and reflect on the impact your departure would have upon those who survive you. How would the lives of those who survive you be different? How would the course of history be altered without you in it? Focus on the lives you have touched and what you have done for your family, friends, co-workers, and community. Focus on the lives you have not yet impacted and what that loss will mean to them. Imagine your dreams and goals going unrealized and the effect it would have upon your family and others. Make a list of activities or endeavors that you had hoped to experience during your lifetime and assess what their value is to you. What is their value to others? Then, imagine never again checking an accomplishment off that list. What lives have you touched, in what way, and how are those people now different because of their interactions with you? Maybe due to humility or objectivity, we rarely place the same value on our own lives and abilities as others place on them from their perspective. You are valuable.

How can you increase your value to yourself and others?

Spend more time focused on being someone, not something. As a society we are so caught up in striving to be the best at something that we forget to focus on becoming the best person we can be. Start by placing God, your family, those you love, and your own mental and physical health at the top of your priority list. Spend more time focused on reaching your dreams by accomplishing your goals. Your dream might be to get yourself into top physical condition and have a more appealing appearance, while your initial goal might be to lose five pounds within the next two months and engage in some type of physical exercise or cardiovascular workout at least twenty minutes every day. Develop a written plan of action to achieve both, but focus on only one personal, one professional, and one spiritual goal at a time to avoid becoming overwhelmed and discouraged. Author and motivational speaker Curtis Zimmerman points out that "the difference between a dream and a goal is that a goal has a deadline. You are much more likely to accomplish your goals, exceed your expectations, and appreciate their value if you write them down as it makes them real." You will become more consistent, reliable, confident, and accountable when you have something to read and follow that articulates your dreams and goals.

Commit to increasing your mental and emotional capacity and never stop learning. Do this by reading books that stimulate and challenge you and that may elicit a myriad of emotions. Make a list of current interests or concerns and use this list to search for library books to read gratis. Create something literary or more materialistic in nature that is uniquely you. Volunteer your time for someone less fortunate, and dare to learn a new skill, such as a sport, computer program, or a musical instrument, and then teach that skill to others. Focus your time and energy on those in your "tribe," meaning those who are closest to you and involved in your life on a regular and consistent basis. Make them feel valuable by treating them as if they are. Do things that are valuable.

How do you make yourself feel more valuable?

To gain the respect of others, treat yourself with respect. Take your job seriously and work hard. Take care of yourself by eating well and working out. Place the people who truly matter to you as a top priority in your life and make time for them. Schedule time alone for reflection and refueling. Consistently work to lessen or eliminate your limitations and you will quickly gain the respect of others and feel more valuable. The easy way is not to raise yourself up, but rather to put someone else down. It is a contemptible and lazy shot that ultimately makes *you* feel cheap. Do not succumb to this temptation. It will make you appear shallow to others and you end up feeling valueless yourself. If you enjoy belittling others then realize this is a bullying behavior that harms others and harms the bully as well. At times, the truth hurts but always be honest and never gossip. Gossiping is like throwing manure upwind on a blustery day and hoping that it doesn't return to smack you right between the eyes. Everyone is valuable.

Assessing the Value of Relationships

At the most basic level, the value of a diamond is judged by the four C's: cut, clarity, color, and carat. When looking at the people and relationships in your life, use the four C's to measure value but use these four: character, conviction, consistency, and concern.

Character is measured by the decision that you make when you are absolutely, positively sure no one is watching or listening to you. You find a wallet with hundreds of dollars in cash inside, many credit cards, and several forms of identification. The decision you make as to what to do with that wallet defines who you are.

Conviction is your willingness to stick to a plan of action or belief despite pressure from others or the potential consequences involved.

Consistency is achieved when you repeat an action time and again that proves your love, reliability, dependability, and character without a loss of quality, and while meeting all timelines.

Concern is the empathy and care you show for others on a regular basis and indicates your willingness to place the needs and desires of others before your own.

Have Confidence to Make the Right Choice

We all routinely have difficult decisions to make regarding the relationships in our lives and we need to be able to make these choices without second-guessing ourselves. The criteria used to make life choices may be more subjective than those you would use to purchase a diamond, but they serve to focus our thinking. Ask yourself, is your life better or worse off because you interact with a certain person on a regular basis? Is there an obvious reason why this person is involved in your life or is the rationale a bit subtler?

Your value and the value of others are not things to which a dollar figure can be affixed. That is called net worth and has little to do with who you are as a person. To make yourself and others feel more valuable you need to follow Elon's lead and learn from the teachable moments in your life. Our value is measured by how we treat ourselves and our families, how we contribute to our jobs, God's plan, society, and all of nature as well as the impact it would have upon others if we were absent from their lives forever.

*YOU WON'T FIND THE RIGHT PERSON
UNTIL YOU BECOME THE RIGHT PERSON.*

— Dennis McCallum and Gary DeLashmutt

CHAPTER 3

Be Respectful

A woman walks out of an ice cream store with two cones and hands the larger one to her companion. One person patiently waits a moment and holds a door open for another. On a busy shopping day a young man yields a parking spot to a woman with children although he arrived there first. Or a gentleman walks around and opens his friend's car door first. When we witness such selfless actions we usually conclude that these individuals are respectful.

Occasionally we are privileged to see respect played out on a grand scale. Most of us can easily open a door, share an ice cream cone, or cede a parking spot, but it takes a person with a servant's heart to put her own life on hold in deference to another person's life and well-being. That is exactly what Gail did for many years as she cared for her mother, Vivian.

Identifying Selfless Love and Respect

Gail was attending college and on her way to lunch when she got a call that changed her life. Her mother had just experienced a massive stroke and Gail was asked to come to the hospital immediately. Fortunately, her mother was a nurse and experienced the stroke while on duty, so care was immediate, but the prognosis was not hopeful.

Gail's mother underwent a dangerous and lengthy surgery. The family's stamina, faith, and conviction were taxed, but her mother survived. From that point on, however, life changed in the family and Gail took on many responsibilities. She received some assistance from loving family and friends, but for the next few years the bulk of her mother's day-to-day care fell to Gail. She handled all the medical appointments, complex prescriptions, and diet. She fed her mother, pureed her food when she was unable to swallow, talked and sang to her, held her, prayed with her, and even changed her diapers when she became incontinent. When her father became ill years later, and eventually passed away, the expectations multiplied. She never returned to college, but Gail will tell you to this day that what she did for her parents was a labor of love.

Respect is shown by people who show

appreciation and admiration for another person while holding him or her in high esteem. Truly respectful people treat others with dignity because they believe in the worth of every person. Treating others with respect is not a coincidence. It is learned behavior that is ingrained in us from childhood when we are taught by people who care about us, such as parents and teachers, to be polite, courteous, and mindful, to think of others first, and to remain alert to our surroundings and situations that may develop and require a respectful reaction.

People like Gail serve as respect role models for all of us. Love played a part in shaping Gail's behavior and decisions, but respect for her mother and for her quality of life in her declining years was at the forefront. She sacrificed many aspects of her life to improve her mother's quality of life. We need to remember people like Gail when we meet disrespectful people.

Disrespectful people are easy to spot because they act as if they just don't care. They cut you off in traffic, gossip uncontrollably, grope and fondle each other in public, talk too loud in movies, use profanity in the presence of children, and fail to return items that they borrow. They live their lives focused solely upon themselves and are completely oblivious to others.

Increasing Disrespect

There seems to be a dramatic rise in disrespectful behavior. People want what they want and they want it right now. This has led to discourteous, impatient, and belligerent behavior especially aimed at service personnel such as waitresses, flight attendants, store clerks, and vendors. People are wearing less and less clothing in public. Does the public want to know the color of someone's boxer shorts or thong or be exposed to a ring in a navel? I have yet to find any of these to be an interesting topic of conversation. Young couples are engaging in heightened PDA (public displays of affection). There are times while walking through a park or down the corridor of a mall that I feel the need to shield my daughters' eyes and suggest to the couple that they get a room. Excessive PDA makes observers feel uncomfortable or even embarrassed. Polite etiquette needs to return. Words such as "please" and "thank you" have become rare courtesies. "Yes ma'am" and "No sir" are extinct phrases in some parts of the country. Many of our youth mock and laugh behind the backs of our elderly when they cross paths. A growing number of cell phone users seem to consider public places to be their personal spaces in which to talk loudly, excessively, and provocatively with little regard to those around them. This is "privacy pollution" and I wish I could call the "privacy police."

Some people do it for the attention. Others simply don't realize or don't care how loud, obnoxious, and conspicuous they act. They seem oblivious to others who can't help but listen as private conversations are made public. Certain people may know exactly what they are doing and get a spike in self-esteem just knowing that they have an audience for their self-perceived business savvy, wit, or intoxicating sexuality. This is not only disrespectful to people within physical listening range but also to the person on the other end of the line who probably has no idea that their conversation is being broadcast to a larger audience. Sadly, a person who is openly disrespectful in public is likely to be someone who has not earned respect in private settings such as at home or in his or her relationships on the job.

The point is that people who are disrespectful of one another are selfish. They focus on their own needs, desires, and feelings without regard to everyone else's. These privacy pollution violators provide us with a clear indication of their character. Have we forgotten that respect is a willingness to show consideration or appreciation of others? That it should be mutual, equal, and earned? Too often, perhaps with the media's help, we come to believe that respect is automatically bestowed upon people with the most money, the fastest retort, the whitest teeth, the most perfect physique, the largest house, or the most notoriety.

Have We Become Numb?

Perhaps talk shows, reality television, movies, magazines, and newspapers have desensitized people to what it means to have respect for others. Have we lost our value for privacy? No topic or method of disclosing it seems to be taboo. Every human feeling, thought, and behavior, no matter how dysfunctional, is out in the open for all to see, hear, and experience "as it happens." I think this mentality is bleeding over into and harming our personal relationships.

A wealthy self-centered person may not be the most enjoyable company. The person with a perfect body and sex appeal may have only one friend—his or her paid personal trainer. Mutual respect is not based on what we own or how we look; rather, those of integrity and character— those who are loyal, dependable, and appreciative of one another—consistently earn it over time. Respect is bestowed upon those whose words and actions show they are consistently mindful and considerate of others.

It is easy to differentiate between respectful individuals and those who take a "me first" stance. A respectful individual is intentionally thoughtful and attentive to others as a part of everyday life. This means considering the effects that each and every decision we make has upon the lives of those around us. Our decisions and actions profoundly affect others and ourselves. We need to be conscious of how our decisions may alter how we see ourselves and how others view us, as well as our relationship with God and the people in our lives.

Mutual Respect

Remember that respect is mutual. This means that we deserve to be treated with the same level of respect that we give to others. Every day spent in a relationship or interacting with someone who is disrespectful to you causes negative consequences to transpire:

1.) You *will* lose valuable self-esteem, which takes consistent and conscientious effort over time to repair and regain.

2.) You *will* begin to believe that you don't deserve more respect than you are receiving.

3.) You *will* learn to settle for the way things

are. You *will* become convinced you are getting at least the same or more respect than the average person, and thus should be grateful and live with what you have.

If you sense a lack of respect in your relationships, believe it. According to relationship expert Alarie Tennille, "being mindful involves the extraordinary nature of day-to-day love and respect. Day-to-day love is about the little things that make a couple unique." Respectful relationships manifest themselves in many ways: a few chosen words spoken at the right moment, a quick kiss that means more than words, the squeeze of a hand, a warm embrace, or the gentle caress of a fingertip. It's a glance or a hug held for one extra emotional moment. It's a sincere "I'm sorry" relayed after a disagreement. It is eye contact between parents and children during a school play or when a youth choir sings. It's a loving message left on an answering machine or the way two people unconsciously complete each other's sentences.

Couples who respect one another are linked in countless ways that none of us can fully comprehend. This includes the admiration, dependability, loyalty, and generosity that occur instinctively every day. They have memories of actions and words to remind them of a partner's unconditional love. Unconditional love eliminates preconceived notions and expectations. In respectful relationships the daily routine becomes a celebration of being together where every day is special. There is no scorekeeping, no expectation of a reward for a kind gesture or a job well done. Love and respect shows up as heartfelt thankfulness, a smile, or physical passion.

Respectful lovers take the time to make considerate choices and never cast judgment when their partner makes an honest mistake. They understand that a loving relationship is a choice and anything in life worth having is worth working for and there is no doubt that successful relationships take hard work. The hard work that sustains relationships is both mental and physical. There is compromise, the sharing of responsibilities, holding your tongue when a situation warrants, and looking for the positive when none seems present. Relationships take effort but the return on your investment is worth it.

When I listen to people talk about relationship problems I often hear a recurring theme: "They must not love me anymore because they don't say it as often as they used to." We all know how comforting and empowering it is to hear the words "I love you." Conversely, the absence of these words can signal a shift in emotions and alter the status of a marriage or relationship. Just because the words are absent, however, it doesn't mean that the feelings are as well and people need to take a moment to reflect upon their entire relationship before jumping to conclusions that may or may not be true.

Another tactic that can destroy relationships is called counter-dependence—a sometimes-transparent disguise for a damaged self-esteem. Counter-dependence is a control strategy whereby one person attempts to meet his or her own needs and desires by making another person feel guilty and responsible for fulfilling them. A counter-dependent person places blame on others for aspects of his or her life that are missing or dormant. A significant other may be manipulated into coming to the rescue and responds out of fear of being labeled uncaring, thoughtless, or unsympathetic. Conversations exhibiting counter-dependence may include the following conditional sentences:

- "If you really loved me, you'd tell me more often."
- "If you were truly committed to me and this relationship, we'd be having sex by now."

- "If you thought we really had a future, we'd be living together by now."
- "If you trusted me, you would have given me the money without asking what it was for."
- "If you really knew me you would know what I was thinking."

A truly conscientious and respectful person does not use this kind of if-then unhealthy strategy, as that type of person knows that any results they obtain from it are tainted and unnatural.

People who truly love each other don't need to say "I love you" a certain number of times per day. Nor do they keep a tally to make sure they are receiving as much from the relationship as they are putting in. There is no question that it is special to hear a heartfelt and passionate "I love you" from someone you love. In fact, there is nothing more satisfying. But if the words "I love you" are scripted, emotionless, or expressed out of obligation they can leave the recipient feeling patronized, demoralized, depressed, and hopeless. The words "I love you" should not be spoken to appease. They should be spoken because they are sincere and meaningful.

Of course there are many sentiments that are

shared in a healthy relationship. Couples who respect each other remember to express a heart-felt thank-you. They give loved ones physical and mental space when they sense a break is needed. Healthy lovers observe needs and wants in loved ones and reverse the roles at home when there is tension or monotony. When needed, they help their loved one escape from their everyday routine and lifestyle and provide a much-needed physical, spiritual, and emotional vacation. Healthy relationships are reciprocal. There is a natural give and take that is not demanding, expected, or forced in any way.

Respectful people often find themselves in healthy, loving, and passionate relationships, because in working to become the right person, they attracted the right person. As they grow as a couple and continue to practice respectful behavior they become the type of role models every family and community needs to perpetuate the right actions and eliminate the negative behaviors that are making society less respectful. Be respectful of yourself and others and release yourself of relationships that are otherwise.

*ELEPHANTS AREN'T THE ONLY
ONES WHO NEVER FORGET!*

— David Coleman

CHAPTER 4

Be Forgiving

I have learned over the years that people forgive but they rarely forget and life can sometimes seem unfair. For instance, why do my sisters continue to remind me (and anyone who will listen) that as a very young boy I used to embarrass them in front of friends because I would run around the house in my underwear, robe, and knee-high black boots pretending to be Batman? Why does the subject of laundry with my wife always end with her recalling the loads where I threw unsorted laundry into the washing machine and the whites came out pink or the sweaters shrunk? Why does one of my friends always remind me of the money he had to loan me when we were nearly out of gas and in the middle of nowhere? And, why is it that a relationship or marriage, which has taken months or years to grow and develop, is destroyed (often permanently) over a casual remark or slight indiscretion? It all comes down to forgiveness and acceptance. The people in the former examples forgave but did not forget—people in the last example simply never forgave.

These were all moments in time...well, the desire to be Batman lasted a few months...but still a moment in time. These moments are like videotape, forever captured in time. They remind me of the courtroom scenes on television or in a movie, during which one lawyer will pose in front of the witness on the stand, raise an eyebrow as music swells, and cross the "line of acceptance" during questioning. Immediately the judge directs the jury to "disregard that last statement (or sequence, or answer) in its entirety. You are to give it no credence when deciding the merit of this case." Most of us sarcastically think, "Oh sure, judge, they will just forget it. Poof, it's gone. They will never think of it again." We all know there is no way the jury will totally disregard information so revealing.

The same holds true regarding arguments between people. For example, a "discussion" with a friend, spouse, lover, or co-worker gets increasingly more intense until someone blurts out a statement that she or he would immediately like to take back. We grasp at the words as they travel through the air in a desperate attempt to shove them back down our throat before they fully escape—but it is too late. You have heard them and perhaps said them yourself. "I've always thought that your sister was more attractive than you." "You were always Mom's favorite." "You're such a jerk." "Quit whining, you spoiled brat." "No wonder she left you." "It's not hard to see why you are still single." "Yes, you do look fat in that dress." "What was I thinking when I married you?" "You really are horrible in bed." "You kiss like a lizard." "At least I did something with my life." Sometimes the words hang in the air like a storm cloud that simply won't dissipate.

We have all expressed thoughts or feelings that we later regret. We may talk before we think, when we are extremely angry or under tremendous duress. Yet seldom does this excuse the words or action. The emotional damage is done. Can an apology correct a mistake? If the victim is willing to receive a sincere expression of regret, then this can start a relationship repair. But we can never fully take back what we have said in anger. Words leave a lasting imprint and reveal character truths. The receiver of a hateful verbal barrage knows that at the peak of frustration we often show core personality traits.

The receiver often gives statements made under such circumstances more weight, as he or she believes that the truth finally came out, creating feelings of shame and guilt in the speaker. It is at this point where the receiver must consider forgiving the sender even though he or she may never forget the message.

Blocked Goals

Renowned Christian self-help author Neil Anderson, Ed. D., in his marvelous book, *Victory Over the Darkness,* defines anger as "a blocked goal." (pp. 126-127) When we become angry, it often is not the person we have a problem with, it is the fact that in some way he or she is blocking a goal that we hope to achieve. For instance, think about the feelings behind these statements: "You are such a slob! Were you born in a barn? Didn't your mother teach you anything about cleanliness? You must not hear a word I am saying or not care because you keep doing the same thing over and over again."

What is being expressed is the blocked goal of having a neater, more organized environment, with less unnecessary work. This goal is being blocked by another person's lack of cooperation. The objectionable behavior is acting as a deterrent to the angry individual's goal. Maybe the person is a complete slob and this behavior makes him/her seem uncaring and unsympathetic. But messiness doesn't necessarily indicate that this is a person of low morals or bad character. Unfortunately, the angry person has attacked a mother, intentions, and perhaps even the ability of the recipient to have a healthy relationship, all of which can be forgiven but not necessarily forgotten.

If this was a wife angry with her husband, she had every right to feel ignored and to express her displeasure at her husband. However, she did not have the right to attack his mother, character, and motives. What's more, doing so is destructive to the relationship and unproductive in solving the problem. When we are dissatisfied with someone's actions or thinking, we need to tell them so, but stick to the facts and keep derogatory comments and vague statements out of the conversation. It is not helpful to attack the person's character. It is helpful to describe the specific behaviors that are seen as a problem. The use of "I-statements" has long been helpful and basic to problem solving. For example, in the situation above, the wife could indicate her stance by saying, "I desire to keep the house clean and you are throwing your dirty clothes on the floor. Please put them in the hamper to help me."

She has expressed her goal, the opposition she is receiving, and the effort that her husband can make to help her successfully maintain the house, and she did all of this without attacking his character or family.

People of integrity don't engage in character debates. The moment you attack another person's integrity you had better be ready for your own character to be put on trial and cross-examined. In the example above, the man can make a concerted effort to be neater and more thoughtful, but the woman can never take back those sentiments she expressed in anger about him, his mother, and his intentions. She can apologize, and her husband may accept the apology, but he may never forget what she said. As healthy adults, we can graciously choose to forgive each other, change behavior, and move forward with the relationship. Forgiveness is a choice and an action that positively impacts both the apologizer and the recipient. Forgetting is not a choice. In fact, trying to forget may actually cause the memory to be made more vivid through rehearsal!

Give It Up...For You

Dr. Anderson defines forgiveness (pp. 201-203) as "giving up the right to hurt someone who has previously hurt you." This is a simple and eloquent way to explain an important and complex principle. It takes a quality person to turn the other cheek instead of slapping the one placed in front of him or her—a cheek the person feels he or she has every right to smack. Asking for forgiveness is something that you do for yourself—to relieve yourself of the burden of negative feelings like revenge towards another. It is also something you do for others as they may wonder what they could have done to lead you to such an outburst or how they could be so wrong in their previous perceptions of you. Asking for and receiving forgiveness allows for learning, closure, and growth. It often leads to intense feelings of passion and compassion for both parties as burdens of hurt and guilt are lifted and replaced with honesty, support, and care. The husband discussed earlier could apologize to his wife for his being so sloppy, uncaring, and unappreciative of her efforts. This may lead them to feel much closer than before and united in a new goal.

Think First...Speak Later

The point is that we must think before we express ourselves. We accomplish this by maintaining control over our emotions with strategies like taking a deep breath and counting to ten before responding or taking ourselves away mentally for a few moments to a place that relaxes us, like a beach or ocean. Sharing or knowing every thought and emotion is not always beneficial. For example, in the comedy movie *What Women Want*, actor Mel Gibson develops an ability to hear in real time what women are thinking about him, about life, about everything. It proves to be fun and exhilarating at first. But then he experiences how personally harmful it can be to hear what people actually think and feel about him and what an invasion of their privacy his eavesdropping is. His "power" provided him with an unfair advantage over others that ultimately led to his downfall—he lost his job and his friends and nearly lost the woman of his dreams.

Personal thoughts and feelings are meant to be just that—personal. Gibson's character failed to understand that personal privacy gives us inner peace. We have permission to hold conversations, meetings, or parties with ourselves without inviting anyone else to attend. It is our event with a guest list of one—our private chat room. It is vitally important that we accept that others need to be afforded the same luxury. Just because you haven't been invited into someone's chat room doesn't mean that you are not important to that person. Complete disclosure of all thoughts is not necessary in healthy relationships and can be harmful. Inner or personal thoughts allow us to explore possibilities. These possibilities may be shared later but they allow us to work through problems without burdening or handicapping others. People don't need to apologize or seek forgiveness for wanting to be alone with their thoughts. Indeed, we all need to do so regularly.

Personal thoughts expressed in anger usually cause harm, and asking for forgiveness will sooner or later be necessary. To avoid the need to ask for forgiveness, we need to learn to control our emotions and hold our tongues. The forgiven can release the wrongdoer and escape the paralysis caused by holding a grudge. But when we keep vengeful emotions pent up inside, they wage war upon our character, poke holes in our soul, and cheapen our lives. Why waste a moment on anger that could have been spent on love? We have the opportunity to choose our attitude every day and must educate ourselves that forgiveness is a choice, not a right or privilege. In addition, we should remember the old adage that what goes around, comes around. If we throw something into the wind on a blustery day, we had better be prepared for it to come back at us. No one can live a perfect day or perfect life. We all need to work to understand the concept of forgiveness and put it into practice. One way to do that is to remember that we have all been wronged and we have all wronged others and that both will happen again.

If someone does attack your character, there is no question that it will hurt. But we can control only two things in life: our thoughts and our actions. Figure out what goal is being blocked. Try to learn from it and rectify it by stating your needs calmly and honestly. Empathy, placing yourself in another person's situation and trying to think as that person might, is needed to understand the blocked goals of others. This can initiate a change in your life and help others make changes in theirs. At some point we all need to appropriately confront offenders, forgive them, and move on. And before you say "I can't do that Dave," remember this—saying "I can't!" means "I won't try!" We seldom get a second chance to do the right thing so take advantage of your first opportunity.

In Conclusion

To form a strong relationship, we need to forgive the past transgressions of others and acknowledge that there will be more in the future.

We need to understand that we, and they, are human. We have and will continue to make mistakes. To mend a relationship that may be fractured, we can practice being humble, admit our faults, and cast less judgment upon others. To sustain a relationship, we should refrain from keeping track of who made the most or most recent mistakes, learn to forgive, and move on.

ALL MEN DIE. SOME MEN NEVER LIVE.

— William Wallace

CHAPTER 5

Be Passionate

Passion is present in a relationship when you would rather be with someone more than anyone else in the world, not just to engage physically, but to talk, to tell a good joke, to share some news, to compete, or just to have a listening ear, a real listening ear. Passion can be a positive uniting force.

There are three types of passionate and loving relationships: Eros (physical), Agape (heartfelt) and Philia (friendship). Which ones are you involved with? It's important to know because passion is not to be confused with infatuation or obsession. These are one-sided relationships, in which brief periods of euphoria lead to short-term failure, not long-term success and satisfaction.

I learned about relationships, but more importantly I learned about passion in the eighth grade during basketball season. My eighth grade basketball coaches were Dale and Paul Barcus, two young, dedicated, and ambitious brothers. To the players on the team, they were known covertly as the "Barcus brothers" but overtly as "Coach." They were calm and quiet men until it was time to coach basketball. Basketball and coaching released their spirits, and their inner drive exploded like a Fourth of July celebration. They loved coaching and positively affecting the lives of young men. They sincerely believed that by training young men to do their best on the basketball court, those same young men would be driven to do well in all facets of their lives. They taught us to be team players, and that we could get more accomplished as a team, but they also taught us to be passionate on an individual basis. Each of us had certain skills such as shooting, jumping, rebounding, defense, or passing the ball. They taught us to be passionate about a particular skill and work to perfect it to benefit the team as a whole. The Barcus brothers wanted us to be better, do better, and know why it was important for us to grow as young men. We respected them as coaches and looked to them for guidance. The relationship with them was both Agape and Philia. We sensed that they cared for us from their hearts and felt that we were probably forming friendships that would last a lifetime.

We practiced every night after school and the coaches encouraged us to prepare on our own in our spare time. So we played pick-up games at parks and rebounded for each other's errant shots long after the sun had set. Our first game of the season pitted us against an urban inner city school with a reputation for hard-nosed play. Our yellow bus pulled into the parking lot of a school three times the size of ours. The place was huge. We all commented, from the safety of our bus, that these guys looked bigger, stronger, and meaner than any kids we ever saw at home.

The opposing team took control of the tip-off and scored within seconds. From that moment until the final buzzer sounded, they wiped the floor with us. We were never in the game. It was obvious to everyone that we were outmatched in talent. What was even more obvious was that we played with no heart, no passion.

After the game ended, the entire team could tell that the Barcus brothers were upset with us. The coaches offered no immediate words, no comments on the game; rather, there was a silent tension in that locker room. We assumed it was because we had lost the game so badly. We were completely wrong. They finally asked us to gather round and expressed that what truly angered them was that we showed no spirit during the game, no desire, no passion for playing, much less for winning. They were disappointed in us! They had never said that before and that's what really hurt. Nothing feels emptier or makes you feel more like a failure than disappointing an adult that you admire and look up to. We waited to be reprimanded. We expected to be chastised and for angry fingers to be pointed in our direction. We were disappointed in ourselves and didn't want to admit what had happened to us during that game. We wanted and needed to improve and we waited for them to tell us how that was going to happen.

But the coaches said very little to us after the game (their nonverbal communication said it all, believe me). They spoke calmly yet sternly in their post-game talk and the few words they shared were instilled in me for life. In summation they said:

"You gave up before you even walked off the bus. Your opponent's mere presence defeated you. Losing in the future is a possible option, but playing without passion is not."

In other words, instead of playing to win, we had all played not to lose. Our coaches' passionate words changed the team that night. They changed us as young men. Instead of getting rest on the way home, we talked about attitude, other teams that lacked it, and how we could and would work together as a team. The Barcus brothers scheduled a practice for six o'clock the next morning to begin our transformation. As a unified and motivated group of young men on a new mission, we proceeded to win thirteen games in a row, many in dramatic fashion. I like to boast that in one of the games I hit nine consecutive free throws in the fourth quarter to secure a victory (I haven't hit nine free throws since). Almost everyone on the team was doing something special to help us win. Several of my teammates sank buzzer beater shots to win games, and we had a tenacious full court press that threw other teams into complete disarray. What changed? We began to believe that if we played with conviction, we could win. We had the desire to be the best and we played with the passion of champions.

Our final game was the championship contest against another intimidating urban inner city squad and we had another sizable obstacle—half of our team had developed severe colds and were feeling weak. Our full court press was not quite as intense as we got winded much easier because players were physically ill. We lost. But this time the scenario was different. Not only was the final score much closer than our other loss, but we had played in earnest determination and with heart. Even in defeat, we held our heads high and walked into our locker room feeling proud. Our coaches knew we played with passion, the fans knew it, the opposing team knew it, but more importantly, we knew it.

Never Compromise Passion

What the coaches instilled in all of us that season was a gut check inventory that can be applied on a daily basis to all facets of life. Living life with passion starts with a sincere desire to reach a goal and live a dream. However, the means to that desired outcome must never compromise a person's integrity or self-worth. For instance, "No hunger is so severe that it justifies throwing away God's will to satisfy it." (The Myth of Romance, p. 16) Passion is a vital part of living and having relationships. Every day that we live without passion, we lose the ability to motivate or be motivated and we get cheated out of living that day to its fullest.

Failed relationships may have caused a

person to lose the confidence to believe that someone can be passionate about that person. What many people fail to understand is that first people must be passionate about themselves. There must be passion in fulfilling personal dreams, in abilities and the desire to transfer and project that passion to others. And passion needs to be shared to prevent infatuations or obsessions from developing. Infatuations are "foolish loves," usually resulting from emotions suddenly stirred. For example, a guy looks at a beautiful woman for the first time and says, "I'm in love." He shares his thoughts openly with his buddy and his buddy places a reality check on him. The buddy points out the ring on the left hand, and the infatuation is lost. What if the guy had not shared his sudden passion? Then the infatuation could have developed into an obsession. The guy thinks about his sudden infatuation, he pictures his future with her, how he could make it happen, and an obsession develops. Obsessions are lonely—they are one-sided and can preoccupy the mind with uselessness and false hope. At a minimum, a person with an obsession will have lost valuable time daydreaming, and at the worst, as with stalkers, the person could lose his or her identity, lose any concept of healthy relationships, and end up in jail.

Passion develops for someone or something. Perhaps a person desires to become wealthy but doesn't have a plan and resorts to purchasing instant scratch-off lottery tickets. A couple of tickets can be fun as the numbers are scratched off. The possibilities and the excitement build until all of the numbers have been exposed. During the process, the awareness is heightened and interest and passion run high. The intensity of the moment reaches its crescendo and then wanes. It will take more lottery tickets to keep this passion alive now that it has turned into an infatuation or obsession. This person needs to share the desire to become wealthy. A good friend will inform that lottery tickets are successful for only a very few people and perhaps offer direction to a new business opportunity that makes better sense. If the passion to be wealthy is not shared, a cycle could quickly develop and a person could become infatuated not with gambling but with the passion of becoming wealthy no matter the method or associated cost. The lack of sharing passion results from fear and perceived accountability. People mostly fear from the following five scenarios. They fear they:

won't get something they want.

will lose something they already have.

will be embarrassed.

will become unnecessary or irrelevant.
will be hurt.

Passion Is Not Short-Lived

True passion is not short-lived. There are
those people who have short-lived desires for a
person or outcome that are perceived as passions
and can do much damage if not kept in check.
The same sometimes holds true for passionate
short-term relationships. Some people like the
stimulation created by the chase more than an
enduring and substantial relationship itself.
These individuals are called "fox hunters." They
see a new relationship as a game to win instant
physical and emotional gratification. But once
the stimulation is gone, fox hunters are off to
the next hunt, chase, and conquest. It is a new
person or situation that piques their interest, and
their hunger can never thoroughly be quenched.

Passion is a wonderful thing to possess and
makes life worth living. It provides us with
marvelous energy and a clear view of what we
want and why. We do need to be cautious of those
who may try to diminish our passion. This desire
to diminish one's passion may result from over-
concern or jealousy. The desire to protect a
person from harm may result in overprotection,

which is just as bad a trait to have as jealousy. Overprotection prevents a person from growing. Jealousy makes people say and do things that are uncharacteristic. Some people are not self-assured. They feel poorly about themselves and consciously or subconsciously begin to suck the passion from those around them. They may do this to relieve the pressure they feel to be something more than they are or in an attempt to feel better about themselves. Their jealousy meter rises. They begin to doubt that there could ever be a passionate person out there who experiences a high level of joy and interest directed at them. Those who lack passion may find themselves making excuses for their lack of passion or attempting to poke holes in the armor of those around them with a zest and zeal for life and living.

Passionate, successful, and motivated people are those who surround themselves with people who react positively to them in relation to others. It is impossible to be and act indifferent around people who enjoy life, who relish each moment and who make their relationships matter without feeling a chasm between what is and what should and could be in life. Passion is available to all who seek it. The secret is trying to find what excites you and feels wonderful.

Passion is easy to identify when you see it. NASCAR driver Dale Earnhardt, Jr. has an obvious passion for car racing. Even though he lost his father to an accident at the Daytona 500, he continues to push to be the most dominant racecar driver competing today. He battles fearlessly with heart and courage. Author John Eldredge has a passion for writing books that change lives. His book *Wild at Heart* changed my life and made me acutely aware of the passions and desires that guide all men. Actress Halle Berry is a passionate actress whose energy and resolve led her to be the first black woman to win an Oscar for best actress and the first black actor of any sex to win (along with Denzel Washington) since 1969. Passion is obviously not short-lived with these people.

The Three Types of Passionate, Loving Relationships

There are three types of passionate relationships found in all healthy relationships: Eros, Agape, and Philia. Eros is the most outwardly evident form of passion revealed in most relationships. Eros love is a powerful attraction and connection between two people who desire each other physically and is extremely important to the overall success and health of a relationship. If we are not physically attracted to a significant other or partner, consciously or unconsciously, we may seek to meet those needs in another person and thus destroy the bonds of trust and respect that are equally essential to relationship success. However, in new relationships, the quicker and farther someone wants to go with us physically, the less likely it is there are any long-term plans. Beware of those who seek a conquest, not a companion.

Pleasure and swift gratification are Eros's staples. A relationship that is based solely upon Eros love is destined to fail. Over time, bodies deteriorate and desires dissipate. The latter may be perceived as a lack of love or conviction by the person feeling neglected and unwanted. If love is based solely upon appearance and attraction, what happens when someone who is better looking or in better shape comes along? No matter how sexy, lovely, or eye-catching we believe that we are, no matter how gifted or skilled we are at lovemaking, someone on this planet is sexier and more provocative than we are. To prove this fact, turn on your television or pick up a magazine. Travel to a tropical resort destination or cruise the streets of New York, Miami, Milan, or Paris and measure your physical attributes against people you encounter.

If we turn love into a beauty contest, over time, we will always lose. Physical passion can wane when a couple allows themselves to surrender to routine and stagnancy permeates their interactions. Passion may also wane when it becomes allowable and no longer novel. In my interactions with people and their relationships, women have expressed to me that men incorrectly boil physical passion down to three categories: French kissing, heavy petting, and intercourse. These women wish more men knew that physical passion could be heightened by focusing on areas of the body that get little attention. Here is a woman's wish list: Kissing fingertips, one at a time, kissing the corners of the mouth, the palm, the back of the neck, eyelids, the crook of her arm, ears, and ear lobes. Rub (not tickle) her feet. Gently scratch her head. Stroke her hair. Rub her back. Do all of these while looking deeply into her eyes with a look of love and admiration, not lust. With the passion of Eros, two persons yearn to be together to feel complete.

Agape love is the love that binds through shared moments. It is a love that is accepting, accommodating, and denies time. It is a love that we choose to send and receive, to sense and learn. Agape partners look for ways to please. The ability for couples to remain passionate is greatly diminished without sincere Agape love. Agape is not based on mere companionship or pleasure but instead on the desire to do what is good for the benefit, protection, and betterment of the person's partner. Agape is working two jobs so the partner can pursue his or her dream of higher education. Agape means automatically swinging your arm against the passenger seat when having to hit the brakes of your car too fast. Agape has the passion to rescue a partner when it may mean putting oneself at risk, such as caring for a mentally or physically sick partner when you may lose all your worldly possessions. Agape is an essential love, especially when Eros love begins to wane or Philia love is taking a vacation.

Agape passion is not to be confused with pampering or idolizing. It is not an intense experience that happens as the result of unclear conditions, the manipulation of feelings, or mental incapacity. Agape is flexible and allows partners to make mistakes, and is still there in the end.

How do you maintain Agape passion? Spend time with your loved ones any way that you can—be it in person, on the phone, or through email, notes, or letters. Long-distance relationships present a skewed vision of passion and love. An old wives tale suggests that absence makes the heart grow fonder. My experience has shown that it is actually proximity that makes the heart grow fonder. The longer someone is out of sight, and as our interactions with him or her become less frequent, the more they grow out of mind as well. We find other ways to fulfill our needs and desires. The people we see on a more regular basis begin to capture our attention and become our primary focus. When a couple first experiences a long-distance relationship, there will often be an immediate rise or spike in passion as they yearn to be together. But over time, they learn to adapt and become more comfortable without their partner. Often, when the couple comes back together after a significant separation, they are no longer as effective together. They have learned to cope and survive without each other. A new pattern and lifestyle developed and became the norm. Lost passion is not easily recaptured as it is never quite as new and novel as the first time it was experienced.

Philia is the love found between good friends. Friends are rare and time spent with them is effortless. In their presence, time seems to pass by quickly. Friends do not keep track of who has been more helpful, has put in more effort, or who has communicated more. They reconnect after a separation or absence as if time had never passed. Friends may disagree and find themselves at odds with each other, but they always find a way to come together and reach common ground. It takes time and effort for people to grow to be caring and loyal friends; thus, it takes a monumental adversity for that friendship to become fractured or need to be terminated.

Passion is an important and essential aspect of life. Educator and professional editor Darline Clemens offers that "passion is about life and it encompasses every aspect of your life, the life you lead, the love of your children, family, friends, God, and the love of life. Without passion, you lose focus and wander in a void."

Until we successfully achieve passion, reach our goals, and satisfy our expectations, we remain unsettled, unsatisfied, and without closure. In relationships, this is the main reason so many people are unable to cope with the termination of a relationship if they didn't initiate the termination. If they were not the one who called a halt to the relationship, they may not be able to experience closure. The ending may have been disconcerting, confusing, and hurtful. A person with passion can recover and transfer passion into a new relationship or endeavor.

We all want and need passion in our lives.

So where, when, and how does it develop? It develops in a resolve to follow your dreams and reach your goals. What is it that you want? A spouse? A job? A career? A hobby? Look at the list of fears that may be holding you back from sharing your passion. Are you afraid that you won't get what you want? You are right. You won't get what you want unless you develop a passion to try. If you are looking for a spouse, identify the qualities you want in someone else, and the qualities that you must have personally? Integrity? Trustworthiness? Height? Education? The desire for children? Are you afraid that you will lose what you already have? Do you have a partner who is noncommittal? Do you have a partner who is abusive? Do you want the situation to continue? If you don't then visualize your passion, make a plan, and go after it. Are you afraid of being embarrassed? Won't you be embarrassed when they find out that you are not passionate in your current situation? Are you afraid of becoming unnecessary or irrelevant? If you are developing a passion for a change, perhaps the question needs to be, "Hasn't that already happened?" And finally, if you are afraid of being hurt, emotionally, mentally, or physically, then get passionate for yourself, and your own well-being. There are places to go, safe shelters for a new life, and a new chance at happiness.

My parents have both passed away and the Barcus brothers have long stopped coaching, but they all taught me well about passion. There are times when I find myself in personal and professional situations where self-doubt creeps into my thinking. I question my abilities and myself and feel a bit apprehensive. When this happens, I take a deep breath and picture my father fishing on the bridge, my mother attempting to speak and walk, or the look in the eyes of my coaches when they said, "Play with the passion of a champion." At that moment I remember the only limitations that I face in life are those I place upon myself. What I have learned is that having passion means that I will never again be defeated before I step off the bus.

WHO CAN ASK MORE OF A MAN,
THAN GIVING ALL WITHIN HIS SPAN?
*GIVING ALL IT SEEMS TO ME IS
NOT SO FAR FROM VICTORY.*

— John Wooden, Legendary
U.C.L.A. Basketball Coach

CHAPTER 6

Be Committed

When I was a young boy, hunting was just starting to become en vogue and be considered a sport. It seemed that every father in our neighborhood was gearing up in orange vests, baseball caps, camouflage pants, and insulated boots. My father, who was caught up in the moment, was no different.

One overcast day in late fall, I recall Dad packing up his shotgun, chewing tobacco, and thermos, and hopping into the car with his friends to hunt big game. Although I was not present as an eyewitness, the following story is now frozen in time as family and neighborhood folklore. Allegedly, my father shot a rabbit. A precious white rabbit with beautiful red eyes, a bright pink nose, and the fluffiest, roundest tail you have ever seen. Dad was sure that he had hit his target and approached the spot where he thought he would find the carcass. Alas, no rabbit. But he did notice a trail of blood. Droplet after droplet, my father followed the bloody path.

After playing bloodhound for half an hour, my father spotted the rabbit. Covered in crimson and barely alive, it was leaning up against the trunk of a small tree. In shock and trembling, it had given up and awaited its fate. You would have thought that my father would have been elated since he had tracked down his prey. But he wasn't. In fact, he was so saddened by the sight of the bloodstained rabbit and so disgusted by what he had done, that he gently wrapped the dying animal inside his coat, brought it home, and began to nurse it back to health. He took some good-natured ribbing from his friends and family, but it didn't matter. He knew he was doing the right thing by being true to who he was.

The next day, he took the rabbit to a veterinarian and had the buckshot removed and the wounds bandaged. Then he bought a cage, filled it with lettuce, carrots, and drinking water and installed a tiny treadmill so that the animal could exercise inside its new rehabilitation center.

After several months of tender loving care, the rabbit appeared to be healthy once again. Dad and I drove out in the countryside and set it free. It hopped out of the cage, momentarily glanced back, and then scurried into the brush. We smiled, got into the car, and drove home in complete silence, alone with our thoughts. The next day, my father sold his gun and never hunted again.

My father was not committed to hunting. In fact he recognized that hunting was in direct opposition to many things he personally believed and stood for. He was for life. Hunting, when successfully accomplished, meant that something would die. He was for a fair fight. To the best of my knowledge, he never encountered an animal carrying a weapon. He knew that hunting was a way of controlling overpopulation, limiting starvation, and keeping animals from damaging crops that farmers worked hard to plant and harvest, but he knew that it wasn't a part of his fiber to be the one who did the weaning. Dad was never vested in hunting and thus it was easy for him to drop it as a hobby and remove it from his life.

Unfortunately, many relationships are formed on the same principles used by a hunter whose heart isn't backing his or her actions. People make verbal commitments to one another before being fully committed and invested. They marry based on infatuation, heat of the moment passion, loneliness, or misplaced hopes for the future, not love. It isn't surprising that many of these relationships fail. When infatuation or passion is mistaken for love and commitment, some make a leap of faith before checking to see if a safety net even exists.

How does this happen? Sometimes people are so busy being something that they forget to be someone. In our immediate gratification-focused society we want everything as quickly as possible without having to invest our time, energy, or money to get it. Unfortunately, that is not the way life works. Anything worth having is worth the effort.

Commitment is the final stage of a relationship. Commitment only results when considerable time and effort have been expended and the parties involved have learned thoroughly about the object of their affection and desire to spend much more time with them in the future.

Commitment is preceded by four other stages: infatuation, discovery, reality, and decision.

Infatuation is the first stage. We catch someone else's eyes, our hearts begin to palpitate, and this person occupies our every thought and desire. The person can do no wrong and we cannot imagine him or her being anything but perfect for us.

Stage two, discovery, is reached when we realize that blind infatuation no longer exists and we accept that the person we find so interesting is human after all and thus has faults. The person may be the wrong religion, use improper English, smoke, or be less than adept at personal hygiene. Whatever the imperfection, we discern that the person is not perfect.

Stage three is reality. We have known and dated this person long enough to know exactly who the person is and where he or she is coming from. Facades no longer work and we have a clear indication of who the person is individually and in a relationship.

The fourth stage occurs when it is time to make a decision. Do we move forward and attempt to make this relationship work and matter, or is it time to call it quits?

Each stage may occur at different speeds, yet each is an important building block. Each is a part of the foundation for a quality relationship.

Divorce and How Men and Women View Commitment

According to The National Center for Health Statistics, "About 50% of first marriages for men under age 45 may end in divorce, and between

44 and 52% of women's first marriages may end in divorce." Basically, this means that out of every ten couples who say "We do," five couples will eventually say "We're through" and call it quits. Unfortunately, divorce affects not only the separating couple but their immediate and extended sphere of influence, which includes children, parents, siblings, friends, neighbors, and co-workers.

My experiences have taught me that quite often men and women view commitment differently. Many men initially see a commitment as a loss of freedom because they have to be accountable to another person for their thoughts and actions. They may believe they have even made a decision that will inhibit their lives. Obviously, many men do marry and commit to relationships and thrive as husbands and fathers. This happens when men are mature enough to see that having the person they love in their lives for a lifetime outweighs any potential restrictions on their freedom or the possibility of meeting someone else. For some, the attraction to a loving partner means the acceptance of change. Men in love can't bear the thought of being without the person they love. This love far outweighs the thought of any boundaries marriage may place upon their new lifestyle.

In contrast, women more often view commitment as a positive addition to their lives. Women look forward to having someone with whom they can share thoughts, experiences, joys, and sorrows. They believe they have made a connection that will enhance life. They also believe that the person they are interested in and the relationship itself will gain momentum over time.

Once a commitment is made, there are three probable outcomes. Often all three outcomes are experienced during a relationship.

The first is that the relationship will improve and grow. This happens as individuals learn more about each other and come to appreciate the unique attributes of one another. The relationship gains momentum as partners discover what it means to be devoted to another person.

The second possibility is that the relationship will arrive at a holding pattern and experience little to no growth. It takes less energy to maintain a relationship than it does to begin or end one and couples sometimes fall into the trap of only putting in the effort required to keep a relationship operating at status quo.

Finally, a relationship may regress and go downhill, sometimes rather dramatically, causing an end to the relationship. In this case it is important to have full closure on the failed relationship; otherwise, it becomes difficult to commit to another person in the future. Full closure is reached when both parties understand and accept why the relationship is ending and agree to certain standards of behavior and communication in the future. This does not mean that wounds have mended or that feelings no longer exist; it means that the couple has made a conscious, mature decision to move forward with their lives. Until this closure takes place, you may keep asking, "What might have happened if I would have stayed with my partner and worked things out? How would my life be different, be better?"

Emotions are like a pie. A pie can only be cut into so many pieces. If your emotions are being consumed in one large slice, other parties involved begin to feel cheated and get smaller and smaller pieces of you. And if there are too many small pieces, you may not have a large enough slice left for yourself when you need it most.

Relationship regressions may result when a commitment is made because an ultimatum was delivered by one of the partners. The person who feels he or she holds the upper hand in a relationship usually delivers the ultimatum.

Unfortunately, this person is often only ready to receive one answer—the one he or she prefers. If and when you deliver an ultimatum you need to be prepared to hear both the answer you desire and the one you don't want to hear, which is usually "No." When ultimatums are introduced it means that both people aren't properly prepared to dedicate their lives to one another, and one person feels pressured into asking for a commitment for fear that he or she will lose the other person if he or she doesn't. Most of the time when an ultimatum is delivered, a commitment is not forthcoming, nor should it be. People rarely hesitate when they genuinely want something and are ready for a lifetime commitment. Ultimatums are frequently used as a way to terminate a relationship, rather than to prolong or strengthen one. When a relationship is healthy, passionate, and headed in the direction of permanency, it feels right. In flailing relationships, proposing an ultimatum spares us the pain and guilt of ending the relationship ourselves. It neatly shifts the blame from "the deliverer" to "the recipient," as the recipient supposedly is to blame for being noncommittal and if he or she says "No," that person has ended the relationship.

Ultimatums

Ultimatums cause conflict, which is not always bad. A couple's level of commitment is not tested during times of prosperity; rather, commitment is tested during times of adversity. When a relationship begins to take great effort to maintain or salvage, then partners' intentions become apparent. No one is ever obligated to stay in a bad or unhealthy relationship; however, all couples who have made a commitment are obliged to consider all possible options and to work diligently to make the relationship work. They owe that to themselves and each other. Compromise does not mean putting up a façade and pretending to be someone your partner wants or needs you to be. Compromise means being flexible and accepting without being taken advantage of. We need to remain 100 percent genuine and let others react to us, as they need to. There is a fine line between being flexible and being someone we are not. When another's words and actions control our self-image, then we are living a lie. Such mental fragility will not lead to a strong, healthy, and committed relationship. It will eventually lead to a crescendo of negative emotions where the truth finally becomes painfully clear.

Commitment is challenged when we are

emotionally, physically, or spiritually harmed by a significant other or our feelings fade away. There are times when a relationship simply needs to come to an end—as the chasm between two people widens beyond repair. Sometimes the people involved have moved to polar opposites and so harmed each other that reconciliation is unlikely. Although hard to accept, the people who will hurt us the worst are going to be the people who know us the best. This occurs because we have invested a part of ourselves in them and they know our areas of vulnerability. They know the buttons to push to elicit our strongest emotions. You cannot make someone love you no matter how hard you try, nor can you make yourself love someone when attraction and interest is absent.

In mathematics, one plus one equals two. In a strong relationship, however, one plus one should equal one. It takes one whole, healthy, independent, and dedicated person, plus another whole, healthy, independent, and dedicated person to equal one fully functioning relationship. This does not mean that partners are totally dependent on each other; actually, it is the opposite that is true. Couples need to retain some individual independence of thought and action to keep the relationship strong. If they become so intertwined, inter-connected, and dependent upon one another, when something is remiss they aren't sure how to stay afloat individually.

What happens when there is no longer a commitment to the person that you married or promised your allegiance, but rather to the extensions that have been created from the relationship such as children, possessions, wealth, or a lifestyle? Initially the commitment must have been strong enough to want to establish connections with those extensions, so it is necessary to discern why the commitment was initially made. What was it that you were seeking? Was it to have the family that you never had or to end your loneliness? Was it to experience a joyous holiday season, to have someone to travel with or talk to?

People rarely commit if they don't have to, in order to get what they want from a person or a relationship. No one offers to pay more at a store than the cashier rings up for the purchase, so why would we expect someone to commit to us if the person is having all of his or her wants, needs, and desires for sex or companionship met without having to make an obligation? Couples should never commit out of obligation. Unfortunately, far too many do just that. Two people may have remained intertwined for an extended time to appease each other, family members, or friends. They commit, and some even marry just because it seems like the right thing at the time.

Why do people stay together out of obligation? There are many reasons. First, they don't want to receive zero return on the relationship investment. People invest time, money, and emotional and physical energy into dating and marriage. It is hard to accept that all that effort and investment are lost and that a partner was just broken in for someone else. Sadly, there are those who also believe that they won't be able to replace their dating or marriage partner and the void will lead to loneliness. Of course, that is false. A person who was able to attract and engage in a relationship, especially for an extended period of time, will find other partners, just as attractive and appealing, if not more so.

To make a quality commitment that will stand the test of time, learn to live by a few simple guidelines. Miriam Hamilton Keare may have said it best when she offered her guidelines for living. They are:

1. If you open it, close it.
2. If you turn it on, turn it off.

3. If you unlock it, lock it up.
4. If you break it, admit it.
5. If you can't fix it, call in someone who can.
6. If you borrow it, return it.
7. If you value it, take care of it.
8. If you make a mess, clean it up.
9. If you move it, put it back.
10. If it belongs to someone else, get permission to use it.
11. If you don't know how to operate it, leave it alone.
12. If it is none of your business, don't ask questions.

These rules are usually prominent on many a kitchen refrigerator to remind family members to keep the house clean. But they can be applied to all aspects of our lives. They certainly apply in committing to relationships, in committing to pursue a goal, and in committing to pursue hobbies, including the sport of hunting.

My father should not have embraced his desire to hunt before he realized what he was getting himself into and the type of commitment required. Before he bought his gear, before he unlocked the safety barrel of his gun and shot the rabbit, he needed to understand what it would take to clean up his mess. The experience was not a fulfilling one. He ended up having to put both the rabbit and his own feelings back where they belonged. Mistakes at the least get chalked up to experience and I am sure that this one did for Dad.

Committing to the right person, hobby, career, or belief for the rest of your life requires an investment of lots of energy and time. We need to try to be sure that the ones we find most compelling in life have the capabilities of offering the same in return.

THE ONLY THING WRONG WITH A
SELF-MADE MAN IS THAT AT
SOME POINT IN TIME HE WILL BEGIN
TO WORSHIP HIS MAKER.

— Unknown

CHAPTER 7

Be Spiritual

From my youth, up through college and even into the early period of my marriage, I could have been the poster child for a campaign called, *Don't Let Religion Happen to You!* I was blessed with a loving family who made me feel as if the world revolved around me, but I was raised in a home where religion was not celebrated. My father was raised Jewish and my mother was raised Catholic. Thus, we reveled in Christmas but never joined a church, we sometimes celebrated Chanukah, which meant at least a present a day for a week, and we rejoiced in Easter, even though I believed the holiday was created to honor a magical rabbit that could lay golden chocolate eggs. My parents experimented with various religious-oriented holidays. The big bonus for me was that no matter what holiday my friends at school were talking about, I could chime in on the conversation and appear knowledgeable. I was never left out of the fun and collected far more gifts than my friends. Life was good, or so it seemed.

Then one day, when I was in my early thirties, I was lamenting to my wife, Diane, that although I had won awards, had a great job, many friends, and a loving wife, I felt dissatisfied. Diane has the gifts of candor and frankness. She identified my problem immediately and informed me that until I placed God at the forefront of my life, I would continue to be dissatisfied. I totally wrote off her opinion and even became a bit belligerent. I felt threatened. I responded emotionally, "Religion is a cop-out for people who don't take responsibility for their own actions or responsibilities." I said, "I understand God and spirituality!" I walked out of the room feeling vindicated, but still angry. I know now I was angry because she was right. It was going to take some time for me to reduce my arrogance and refocus my life.

Diane's comments haunted me and eventually made me take a long hard look at how I had arrived at my spiritual destination (a desert). I came to realize that celebrating a holiday is one thing but being spiritually connected to a belief system is entirely different. Celebrating and gift giving is a far cry from living a spiritual relationship with God. Now I understand that spirituality is a never-ending journey, which is an accurate mindset to use in describing human relationships as well. Relationships begin, and once they begin, they never really totally end. I am referring here to all relationships. Some relationships do go sour, but no matter how bad they are, there is still some connection by the fact that there once was a connection. In addition, no matter how fantastic a relationship seems there is always room for improvement. When a relationship is ended through a personal decision, legal means, or by death, it continues to be connected to you through memories and shared experiences. Relationships have a spiritual dimension. They stay with you. They can enhance life in many ways but if nothing else, you can at least say you learned from them. No matter how a relationship ends, once again closure must be reached in order for you to fully move on to new relationships and develop spiritual connections.

Spirituality in Five Components

Spirituality can be broken down into five components. While each stands on its own merit, the five aspects are stronger and more formidable when they function in concert. The five components are hope, faith, love, belief, and obedience.

Hoping is like wishing except there is the expectation that what you want, can and will happen. Hope is based in thinking there is likelihood for what one desires to become a reality. You may hope that a loved one who is quite ill gets better quickly or hope that you become financially successful or hope to be married to a wonderful partner for a lifetime.

Faith is a confident belief in the truth, value, or trustworthiness of a person, idea, or thing. Faith is not tangible; you cannot place your hands on it, and it does not rest on logical or scientific evidence. You are loyal to something or someone and pledge to remain that way whether ever proven unconditionally to be true or not. For example, you may have faith in God, faith that the solar system will stay on track, that the seasons will change, that the rivers will flow, or you have faith that a relationship experiencing difficulty will eventually work out. Christians, Jews, Muslims, and countless other religions have faith in a God they cannot physically see or touch. Faith involves a lifelong search for meaning and truth. A person's faith is a part of the core values they hold. When those core values are in direct opposition or one person in a relationship has faith and the other does not, it may be difficult for a couple to compromise and make tough decisions. An incongruous outlook creates a couple that is unequally yoked.

Love is a deep, tender, and indescribable feeling of affection toward someone. You experience an intense desire and attraction for someone and long to be with that person. You desire that he or she be an integral part of your life and no ultimatum or condition is placed upon his or her reciprocation. There is an underlying feeling of closeness and oneness and you long to grow more committed and connected to the person as time passes. You may love God, your spouse, your children, friends, and even yourself. People usually love their parents and siblings. Some say they love their job or career, but there is a fine line between love and preference. Usually, love involves a living thing that has the capacity to love back. We simply prefer things and processes in life that are inanimate or materialistic like antiques, skiing, or one job versus another. Genuine understanding and appreciation of love involves loving those who are similar but also at times loving involves those who differ from us or stand in opposition, as well. Every person has been placed on earth for a reason. To feel love and have it reciprocated is a spiritual blessing.

The fourth component of spirituality is belief. Belief means placing complete confidence in someone or something. There is an absolute certainty of a person's trustworthiness and acceptance of his or her actions as valid. The belief may be in God, in a supreme entity, being in control, or that attending church makes a person more connected spiritually.

Finally a spiritual person is also obedient. Obedience causes us to comply with and carry out the wishes of others for a variety of reasons. It means relinquishing power or authority and trusting another's judgment to do things the way they should be done. Over time, we obey parents, teachers, and the law. Obedience is giving what we can and it can be spiritually rewarding and self-edifying.

These five components are delightfully and complexly intertwined to form the components of spirituality. Each guides our thoughts, actions, and decisions and together they create an approach to life and relationships. This was made clear to me during a recent time of crisis in my family.

On a recent family vacation to Hilton Head Island, South Carolina, my father in-law experienced chest pains. We rushed him to a local hospital. Very quickly he was diagnosed with a major blockage in one artery. Fortunately, through the miracles of science, he was treated, using a stent to correct the obstruction. He was back out on the beach and with his family within days.

But during those few days, our family experienced several dimensions of spirituality. First, we had to have faith in the doctors and nurses to do their best for my father-in-law. We were not capable of treating him ourselves, so we had to have faith that the medical team could. Those of us on vacation had to have faith and others who were far away had to have faith. I recall one of our teenage family members in Ohio took it upon herself to assure the rest of the family members that "Grandpa will be fine and that he is in good hands with all of us that are caring for him." She had faith from a distance.

Second, our faith transferred into hope and belief. We had hope and belief because my father-in-law was only 64 years old and in good health. We believed that we would spend many more years with him. We had hope and belief that he was strong enough to pull through and he did. We had faith in the hospital to care for him and we believed that our prayers would be heard.

Of course we thought about how much we loved him, as we considered life without him. In the process we also realized how much we loved each other. As we waited for the results of the operation we became closer as a family. We prayed together. We were humbled. We were hospitable to one another and comforted each other as much as possible. We compromised and gave selflessly. Adversity and crisis often forge bonds and break down barriers that become meaningless when someone's life is threatened. Finally, we were obedient and put our faith in God as the fate of our loved one was out of our hands.

Faith, hope, love, belief, and obedience are vital in relationships with others and in the growth of relationships. We must have faith in ourselves, and our commitment to be involved with another person, and we must have faith that the other person will be honest, loyal, and trustworthy. We must have hope for the future and believe that our partner will be there for us as the relationship grows. This hope gives us excitement and anticipation as we consider the future. We must have love. It is the greatest blessing of the five. It is unselfish and other-centered rather than self-centered. It is love that will cause us and the other person to grow and become the people we were destined to be. Motivated by love, we desire the best for those we love. Through it, relationships prosper. We need to believe that we have made the best decisions and choices we can and pledge our allegiance and obedience to God and others in whom we have committed relationships.

Developing Spirituality

To develop personal spirituality, find a place and a way to reflect and spend time. Allow a pattern and rhythm to develop. Much like we should have twenty minutes of aerobic exercise per day to increase or maintain our physical health, faith needs a daily workout as well. When complacency and stagnancy become the norm, temptations arise and cause disruption in your life forever.

Here are a series of spiritual questions to ask on a daily basis. They will help you assess where you are, where you want to be, and how you can get there in relation to your faith.

- Are you connected or disconnected to God and your faith? If you are disconnected, ask yourself why and what can be done to change that, recognizing that you must have a desire to change it. If the desire is lacking it could be because you are just going through the motions to appease your conscience or satisfy your significant other, family, or society.

- Have you spent time alone with God to develop or maintain a personal relationship with him? Sometimes people hesitate spending time in solitude with God because they don't know enough about God or don't know enough about themselves and are fearful as to what might be revealed. Have you been created in the image of God or are you creating an image of God?

- Are you handling your relationships based upon the two questions above?

Life is full of obstacles and opportunities that will challenge your faith, confront your spirit, test your love, question your honesty, try your skills, diminish your hopes, and bombard your beliefs. Temptations will abound and encourage you to cut corners or satisfy desires immediately by choosing the easiest available option. Assess each of these obstacles and look at them as opportunities! Opportunities to positively affect your life and keep you headed in the direction that will lead to more spiritually rewarding relationships. A spiritual person realizes that the journey of life is even more important than the destination because the journey hones a person's character.

Review the previous questions, keeping in mind which argument is winning, the argument for spirituality or the argument against it? Which one is winning, the argument for your relationships or the argument against them? These two questions are intertwined so you may find answers at opposite ends of the spectrum or ones that contradict one another. That's okay because the struggle to mesh diverse perspectives makes life richer. Spirituality allows us to build our minds and bodies so they won't break down under pressure.

Spirituality Demonstrated

Spirituality, or a lack thereof, is demonstrated every day by everyone. Take a moment and observe others. One person may possess a positive, righteous presence and radiate that to others, while another may be obviously negative, false, and void of spirituality. It is when words and actions are inconsistent with beliefs and claims of faith that there is the feeling and appearance to others as hypocritical. Once identified as disingenuous, such a person is no longer seen as a role model or spiritual leader;

rather, the person is seen as confused in the best case and as a liar in the worst. It is important to develop the spirituality within you so that you can discern spirituality in others. We are all human beings. We will all make mistakes, but mistakes can make our faith and spiritual beliefs stronger. Situations change over time, but spirituality based in the five components is meant to be a stabilizer—especially when there are no clear reasons why bad things happen to us or those we know and love. A centering of self helps to build relationships on solid concrete foundations. Relationships that rest on loose sand will quickly erode, especially when constructed near a cliff where danger and self-doubt may lurk.

Spirituality gives the courage to deflect criticism or even persecution from those who disagree with you. That criticism may even take place at home, but can happen at work or even in a social or recreational setting. Spirituality gives a steadfast self-resolve to grow into a more satisfied person who is doing the right things for the right reasons. Of course, there is a fine line between being arrogant and being convinced, so be a role model of your faith, so others will be led to spirituality and not away from it. Taking a "holier-than-thou," "know-it-all" stance may offend everyone, so listen a lot, choose your words carefully, and do a regular self-check on your humility. The minute people assess they are in the presence of a "know it all," they determine that the person knows very little.

Having a spiritual base at home is vitally important and this begins with having a clear leader in every relationship and marriage. This does not mean that one person makes all decisions of a spiritual nature within a home. Husbands and wives often yield such decisions back and forth as knowledge and emotional and personal investment dictate. Decisions can be well thought out and mutually agreed upon, but a strong spiritual, emotional leader needs to be involved in key decisions. This leader makes the tough calls when necessary and when appropriate, and facilitates the difficult discussions when they need to be held. A cocky person or someone who takes advantage in the control position of a relationship cannot handle the leadership role. Rather, spiritual leaders should be ultimate decision makers who rise to the occasion when consensus cannot be reached yet reaching a decision is imperative.

When a couple is truly spiritually connected through a shared faith, then both know that decisions will be based upon common beliefs.

This doesn't necessarily mean that couples always both agree with the choice, but they must agree on how choices are made. Spiritual connectedness is essential in relationships. It does need, however, to be developed by the individual partners, so those two individuals can stand alone when necessary.

When two people are void of faith, they have a weak foundation on which to stand. The success of their choices will be hit or miss and will be much harder to understand. Couples who share hope, faith, love, and beliefs accept the need to be obedient, have a compass for life. They will find joy and satisfaction in praying together, for one another and serving each other without the expectation or need for personal honor.

Your Spiritual Journey

Faith is a choice made with conviction. I am of the Christian faith and it has taken me time to establish a relationship with God. My relationship is not fully developed, but it is started and I intend to continue on my lifelong quest for a deeper, more meaningful relationship with him. What I do have guides the decisions I make in my personal and professional life. My spiritual relationship is the measuring stick for my words and actions. I am not where I ultimately want to be, but I am also not where I used to be. Spirituality, like a relationship, takes time to develop. You need to find a time, a place, and a way to reflect and become more connected to God and your spirituality every day. Allow a pattern and rhythm to develop whereby you assess your dedication to the five components of faith, hope, love, belief, and obedience. Do this and you will find you are well on your way to rewarding spiritual relationships with God and the people in your life who truly matter.

*You cannot change the truth,
but the truth can change you.*

— Unknown

*"If you choose to cheat,
you choose to lose me."*

— Darline Clemens

CHAPTER 8

Be Trustworthy

A few years back, after one of my speeches, I found myself sitting at a table in a restaurant with a half dozen or so of the people who had sponsored and coordinated my appearance. I didn't know any of them well, since I had just met most of them that evening. We had just finished the appetizers when three of the group excused themselves to the lavatory. The three were barely out of range when two individuals who remained at the table began to gossip about them. They criticized their clothes, ridiculed their bodies, and attacked their character. This went on for several minutes until the three returned. I was extremely uncomfortable and wasn't sure what to do. One thing I knew for certain was that my bladder needed to set a world record because there was no way I was going to the restroom until I got back to my hotel room!

Because of those remarks I lost any trust and simultaneously lost any respect that I had held for the gossipers.

I learned a lesson that evening. Most of us want to believe the best about people and human nature, but sometimes we're wrong, very wrong. A person may profess to have a defined level of character, but words and actions will eventually reveal the truth. When words and actions conflict, we will instinctively take the action as the truth.

In the dinner scenario, it was obvious that the gossipmongers eagerly offered their opinions when the objects of ridicule were absent. They did not find similar courage to do so face to face. I could sense that the others at the table, including me, were a captive (and stunned) audience for them. It is the shock factor that gossipmongers desire—to be the one to break the big news and reap attention for being the "source." Sadly, gossipmongers thrive on this kind of attention because they lack certain characteristics.

When looking at relationships it was so obvious that those at the table were lacking at least four of the characteristics present in every healthy relationship. In fact, they could have easily been lacking more but we will focus on the obvious. Those at the table that evening were missing these characteristics: trust, respect, passion, and commitment.

- Trust is confidence that a person's words and actions are reliable.
- Respect is mutual and earned whereby we hold each other in the highest regard because we had past experiences that justify this view.
- Passion is the intense desire to be together physically, emotionally, and spiritually.
- Commitment equates to permanency, is unwavering, and is based upon all of the other relationship elements being in place and functioning successfully.

Relationships Weaken Quickly

When any of the characteristics are absent or weak a relationship will suffer. When trust is the element in question, however, it seems to take on a greater significance and weakens that relationship more rapidly than the others. People rarely show their trustworthiness while in the spotlight. Interestingly, a person's persona is most clearly revealed when he or she feels invisible, invincible, or in peril. This is seen played out by looters who take advantage of a situation like a blackout of electricity. A lack of trust in a relationship weakens the foundation on which a couple operates, communicates, and makes decisions. When trust is shattered, communication may become forced and strained, finger pointing may begin, voices may rise, tempers might flare, and accusations are sure to be leveled.

Common ways people in relationships show they are untrustworthy include lying, cheating, and failing to uphold their end of the relationship by mishandling or ignoring responsibilities. According to noted author and researcher Shirley Glass, 25 percent of wives and 44 percent of husbands have had extramarital attachments.

When we sense that someone is lying to us, we probably are correct. Is this because we are clairvoyant, have a sixth sense, or a heightened sense of intuition? No, it is because we unconsciously or quite knowingly picked up on tendencies from this person that are consistent with lying. People who are being deceptive may avoid eye contact, appear nervous and preoccupied, and tend to blink more often. They may over-explain or over-justify their version of the truth to make sure they said what they wanted to say exactly the way they wanted to say it. The facts and details of the story may change over time or they may begin to modify the story to fit the circumstance or the person they are talking with. A person's manner, style and, delivery of communication quite often change when they are lying. Someone who is normally quiet and reserved may become wordy, or if usually talkative, may seem unusually distant or removed.

As author Kathleen VanHorn advises, "It is a lot easier to stay out of trouble than to get out of trouble." Unconsciously, liars may begin to fidget and play with facial areas, possibly in an attempt to block false words from escaping. They may answer questions with questions or probe for how you found them out so they can try to discredit the source. Often, liars become angry and defensive when being questioned or may laugh off the entire situation as a joke. They develop "selective hearing" and do their best to avoid you without it appearing that way. Out of sight for them hopefully means out of mind for you.

Flirting and lying can lead to another trust breaker—cheating. I have heard as the most common reason people say they cheat on one another is that they get away with it. They cheat on a partner or spouse and this same person takes them back, time and again. While there may be arguments and emotional or physical separations over time, in the end they are taken back and know they got away with cheating. The only way this horrendous cycle of unhealthy behavior and abuse can and will cease is if the harmed person holds fast and forces the cheater to experience actual negative consequences up to and including separation and/or the loss of the relationship. It needs to be said calmly and directly, "If you choose to cheat, you choose to lose me." Cheaters search for someone, anyone, who can fulfill self-perceived needs, voids, and desires. Victims are not hard to find since wounded souls are easy to spot—as their eyes avoid contact, their posture wilts, and they feign smiles that accentuate the pain. Cheaters are blissful with life until the novelty wears off. They may eventually recognize that the problem was deep inside them since the same issues resurface with each new love interest. It just doesn't work to try to get well by making yourself sicker.

Whether they do lose you or not will depend on the sincerity, contriteness, willingness, and ability of your partner to address and handle the situation. In addition, your level of forgiveness, and the spiritual foundation on which you base your decisions, will play key roles in salvaging the relationship.

Another reason people cheat is they have lost trust in one another and use it as a means to retaliate against each other. The problem here, besides the unhealthy behavior, is that an innocent third person has now become involved. These pawns probably do not even know that they are being used in a destructive and pathetic love game of "who can top this and cause the most pain?" It is undeniably wrong to knowingly and willingly use someone for personal advantage in such a relationship tug of war.

Cheating may also develop when passion and intimacy disappear or deteriorate and neither party has the guts to speak up. A couple allows boredom and stagnation to rule their relationship. Often partners don't know how to terminate the relationship.

Healing

When trust is broken, a heartfelt statement of contrition can begin the healing process, but it takes consistent honesty, loyalty, and dependable behavior, over a considerable period of time, before trust can be regained—if ever it can be. To forgive someone who deceives us means that we must juggle our pain, emotions, and fear of appearing gullible. This is done when we still want that offender to remain a part of our lives.

When a person is wronged, it will take time

to heal. To begin the process, it helps to spend time around family and friends with flawless records of faithfulness and impeccable reputations. You need to know what trust feels like again and this will not happen overnight. Your goal, as the person who has lost trust, is to feel and share complete and unconditional trust once again. Think or try imaging a trusted friend. If we truly trust someone, there is nothing we wouldn't share, nor do for him or her. We know this trusted friend would be there for us the instant there is a need. Trust means neither letting others down nor breaking a confidence. We smile when we see those we trust or when they call or write. We have the utmost respect for those we trust and value how rock solid they are. We may marvel at the ease and poise with which they even carry themselves. After this thinking and imaging exercise, you must ascertain whether or not you can ever look at the partner, friend, or family member who has violated your trust as a trustworthy person again.

What Is a Trustworthy Person?

Trustworthy people are that way because they have chosen to enter into a timeless contract with themselves. They agree to live a life full of character, integrity, and truth. It is a life void of deception, coercion, and dishonesty. They find it easier as this is a fulfilling way to live. Spending time with trusted companions is pleasant and effortless because there is no need to be guarded. There is no fear that they will use what you say to hurt you in the future. Your name is safe in their mouth as theirs is in yours.

People who are trustworthy listen to others' concerns and respond with appropriate questions until they obtain understanding. They share ups and downs. They let you rant and rave and then come to your defense, as they help you understand where you have stumbled. They love you for you and sense when you need a gentle embrace or to be left alone. There is a mutual respect for what you each bring to the table. Trustworthy people:

- can laugh with you at your mistakes (or theirs) and cry with joy at your accomplishments.
- give you a comfort level and an ability to simply sit in silence and know that they are there. There is no need to fill silence with words because there is an unspoken understanding that exists on many levels.
- contact you and they will know exactly what to say because they were "just about to call you anyway."

- will catch you if you fall, and practice tough love when it is needed.
- encourage and support and allow you to be silly, creative, or whatever you need to be.
- will allow you to laugh together, real laughter that is impossible to stop, and that takes your breath away.
- are people that you can ask for help and know that you will get it judgment-free.

Being trustworthy is a way of life that you either choose or reject, but it will be impossible to make your relationships matter if you choose the latter. Being trustworthy is for you and relationships that matter, not to satisfy anyone else who may not appreciate nor be able to identify with your integrity.

HAPPINESS IS AN INSIDE JOB.

— Unknown

CHAPTER 9

Be Healthy

I knew many children growing up who battled a problem with their weight, including me. I always carried an extra twenty to thirty pounds that I didn't want, didn't need, and couldn't handle. The weight always seemed to collect around my middle so that it was sure to be noticed. My clothes never fit quite the way I wanted them to and I was a step behind the other kids during recess and when playing sports. Except for an occasional bully who called me "fatso," my life didn't seem to be any worse off than skinnier kids. But as I write about relationships, I have to acknowledge certain relationship(s) that may have contributed to my problem with weight. One relationship is obvious; it was Uncle Frank. To me, he was "Unk" and to him, I was "Davey."

Nearly every day after school, from the time

I was in the first grade until I graduated from sixth grade, my uncle Frank would take me to a fast food restaurant. It was fun hanging out with Unk, who was in his eighties and hailed from Lithuania. He spoke with a bit of broken English, walked bowlegged, and shared his opinion on every topic. He was a wonderfully stubborn man who just couldn't do enough to help our family, especially me. I was the "baby" of the family and he spoiled me. Uncle Frank seemed to be happiest when the "baby" was well fed and satisfied. He was happy quite often.

And so, growing up, one particular fast food restaurant was my nirvana—Burger Chef. It was fun to go with Unk. It was only three minutes from home and had the most delicious food on earth. Back then, nothing was described as "reduced fat" or "light" and no one seemed to care. I liked every food option at this restaurant but I would usually order one of my two favorite meals, either a deep-fried fish sandwich (loaded with lettuce, cheese, and tartar sauce), French fries, and a chocolate milkshake or a triple-decker burger (also loaded with cheese, lettuce, pickles, and sauce), French fries, and a soft drink. Unk always paid but made sure that I ordered it "to go" to avoid paying the eat-in taxes on it. That was okay with me since I figured a penny saved would be a penny earned for future visits to nirvana. Later every evening, I would take my place at the dining room table and eat a full dinner with my family.

As I remember my childhood and times with Uncle Frank, I now know that what seemed like a wonderful, wholesome relationship had some drawbacks. I ate my favorite foods every day, my belly was full, and we would talk and laugh. Years later, however, I am still battling the weight gained at the hands of fast food. I don't blame my uncle. I have had every opportunity to take control of my actions and get myself into shape. It isn't his fault I can't say no. But I want to make sure that I have learned from my relationship with him and don't repeat history. I want to forge healthy relationships with my own family, now that I am the one choosing the restaurants. I want love and respect because I earned it from creating a loving environment, and also a healthy one for my family.

I love my two daughters, Shannon and Natalie. Because of my fast-food-related upbringing, I have trouble telling them "no" when they ask for snacks or extra helpings. But I have learned to say "no," because I need and want them to understand the concept of willpower and the importance of their bodies and their health. An extra twenty pounds is unhealthy. I did that trick, the one where the health teacher has you carry around three five-pound bags of sugar for one day to understand the extra strain weight places on the heart. The "trick" worked and I got the message. I now try to take care of myself and offer healthy tips to those I love and care about.

Physical health and appearance matter in a relationship. Personal appearance is part of the equation because it affects how we feel physically and mentally. Personal appearance does affect self-esteem, self-concept, and confidence. When we feel poorly about ourselves, or a partner, for physical reasons, we may unknowingly harm aspects of the relationship. People who become physically unfit because they lack self-discipline do themselves and their partners a relationship disservice. First, health will decline and secondly, passion and intimacy between partners may diminish. Both place stress on relationships. Physical health is not always reduced intentionally. Medical conditions can cause uncontrollable physical responses. That is not to what I am referring. Keeping physically fit at a minimum means managing your diet and expending time and energy on an appropriate exercise regimen.

Physical health and appearance also play an important role in how attractive we are to others and to ourselves. In American society, judgments about people are frequently based upon personal appearance. It isn't right, or fair, but it is a fact.

It is remarkable what happens to your body and mind when you begin to get yourself in better physical and mental condition. According to personal trainer and health club owner Grey Freudenberg, "When you exercise, your body releases endorphins, a chemical that gives your body a natural high feeling." Not only do physically fit people feel better, they are better off health-wise and they have more energy. Good health and fitness motivate us to make more positive changes and as a result our self-confidence soars. Physically fit people think more clearly and have the capacity to accomplish more in a day. Changes in self-esteem, attitude, and demeanor can be significant and begin to make you appear much more attractive to yourself, and to others. Confidence allows us to approach others or to accept social invitations, which are often more plentiful. As long as an ego spike does not lead to the point of overconfidence or arrogance, your social outlook for the future should be brighter.

It is unfair to label people as shallow or

heartless because they make a personal decision about whom they will and won't date, marry, or interact with based upon physical attributes. I hope everyone will take the time to learn about potential partners on a more personal level. Minimum standards for physical health and appearance in possible partners are at least minimum standards and let's face it, good health will allow more time together. Of course standard setting goes two ways so be aware that others may use those same criteria to measure as well.

Mental health is equally as, if not more important as physical condition when it comes to our relationships, happiness, and satisfaction. Many of us may have problems we are dealing with on an intellectual or emotional level. These problems are not as easy to see as extra pounds and can be disguised or concealed. These problems are potentially more dangerous than those that are more obvious in nature. Mental health requires effort, such as reading, writing, talking, and sometimes it requires a "personal trainer." If problems seem overwhelming, get help. You would be surprised at the number of people with personal counselors. Sometimes we just need someone objective to talk with. It is most acceptable to go to a personal trainer to get physically fit, and it is important to see mental health professionals to get mentally fit if the situation warrants.

Everyone needs someone to talk with openly, someone with whom we feel safe and are confident that we can confide in, not someone who might gossip or use confidences against us in some way. We need people who will hold us accountable for our thoughts, actions, and health, who will not let us put something behind us or suppress it until we have dealt with it properly. The ideal confidante may be our partner, significant other, spouse, or a friend. But we need someone because when a personal problem is suppressed, we become confused, angry, and resentful, which can lead us toward depression, another serious issue. So, we all need to find a safe person to talk with in confidence and one whose advice we will follow because we believe in that person and trust him or her.

A safe confidante may be a professional therapist or counselor, a priest or a pastor, a grandparent, or anyone you consider trustworthy and competent, but you need someone who will focus all of his or her attention on you. A professional can delve into personal issues with you and for you and encourage you to reflect upon and process issues that you may never choose to explore alone. It is important to seek the help needed. It does not make a person appear weak or crazy to ask for and receive the assistance. In fact, it makes people more in control when they accept they have a problem, have found a way to get help, and have begun that process. This is a cleansing, cathartic experience that relieves the burden that has been carried for so long.

To help my daughters grow strong mentally as they are emerging physically, I use a strategy to teach them how men of character act toward women. When they accompany me to dinner, to a movie, shopping, to exercise, or when they join me for a public appearance, I treat them how they should expect to be treated in the future by the men they will date and possibly marry. I open their car door for them. Use polite, appropriate language at all times. Ask them engaging questions during meals and quiet time that require more than "Yes" or "No" answers. I encourage them to talk about themselves and their day and topics that matter to them. I keep them close by when they may feel unsafe and I allow them to order for themselves without feeling any associated pressure that they will be expected to act a certain way or be in debt to me because I took them to a particular place. We observe other couples and share comments. We discuss what it looks and feels like when a man treats a woman with love, class, and dignity and what it is like when a person is being dishonest or disrespectful. The men who date my daughters will be held to a high standard of thought and behavior by two young women who will know the difference between healthy and unhealthy relationships, between right and wrong, and between character and a complete lack there of.

We need to present models to others that are examples of mentally and physically healthy people. These models create a standard for us to apply to others and ourselves. I try to demonstrate healthy, trustworthy, and giving relationships to everyone I come in contact with and look for those who can be models for me. This means that I must also be a character model and admit when and for whatever reason I have failed to live a healthy lifestyle.

As I mentioned, my daughters sometimes travel with me on business or accompany me to public appearances. Once, they were both with me when I was pulled over for speeding. The first thought that entered my head was to do whatever I could to talk my way out of getting a ticket. Then I rewound my thoughts. I knew it would negatively impact my daughters' view of right and wrong if I tried to con the police. This was a chance to teach the concept of being accountable for your actions. I had my driver's license and registration out and available before I was asked for it. When I spoke, I was courteous. I didn't want to teach my children to manipulate others or situations or to become angry or resentful when they were caught doing something wrong. I wanted them to fully understand that there are negative repercussions for inappropriate actions that are legal, healthy, and just. I hope that this is one of many lessons of actions, not just words, that will translate into healthy thinking by them in future relationships.

Willing participants in healthy relationships care about each other physically, mentally, emotionally, and spiritually. That also means sometimes accepting personal differences in one another. For example, my wife, Diane, and I have a few of what some would call role reversal error issues. We each seem to enjoy and excel at roles that are traditionally reserved for the other sex. For instance, I love to cook and experiment with new dishes, while she is indifferent about food and its preparation. She single-handedly remodeled our house and has a much nicer and extensive tool collection than I will ever have. In fact, I must admit that something is sure to end up in even greater disrepair if I try to fix it.

I enjoy shopping and I mean for practically anything at any time. Diane despises most shopping. These areas of difference work out quite well for us, except in the area of music. Road trips can be a nightmare. I like progressive, dance, and trance-like music, while she is an alternative, hard rock fan. We solved the problem by formulating an "I've got the wheel policy." Whoever is driving gets to choose the music being played. Also, having an extra personal compact disc player and headphones available whenever we travel together works in case we reach an impasse.

The wonderful thing about healthy relationships is that the people involved in them do not have to be carbon copy or mirror images of one another. Actually, it works well when two people have different strengths and areas of interests that complement one another. We are attracted to some of the qualities in others that we lack in ourselves.

In a healthy relationship between two people, there must be give and take. At various points one of the persons involved in the relationship will be the stronger person. When the stronger one takes care of the weaker one, without ulterior motive, until the weaker becomes strong on his or her own, the couple is involved in a healthy relationship. When the stronger person takes advantage of the weaker person to keep him or her down, under control, and dependent upon the stronger, the couple is involved in an unhealthy relationship. By "stronger person," I am not referring to the individual with more defined biceps, six-pack abdominal muscles, higher I.Q., more lucrative career, incredible talent, or endless list of friends. The stronger person has the total package of a healthy mind, body, intellect, and life experiences.

At times we need others who are stronger in certain areas to make us strong. There are moments in everyone's life when there is a shortcoming in personality and character. For example, when a store clerk gives too much change, you have to speak up, return the money, and do what is right. Sure, in the back of your mind, you think it would be a buzz to get away with something, share the story with someone, and experience the glory of being "clever." But then you think of your spouse or your children or best friend or pastor and how they would react if they heard you cheated a store clerk. They keep you in check. They are aids to your conscience and your soul. We need these people in our lives.

Along with my wife, I am the head of my

family. It is my job and it is a labor of love to try to make a positive impact on her and my children's lives. I want them to know what a healthy relationship looks and feels and sounds like from someone who loves them unconditionally and dearly. It is only these types of relationships that we should ever allow ourselves to be a part of. Healthy relationships bring out the best in us so we can bring out the best in others. Healthy and successful relationships take work and intrinsically we know how important it is to go the extra mile and make every effort to live every day to the fullest—to make that day of relationships matter.

Mentally and physically healthy relationships share many similarities, which lead to their overall success. Couples divide up and share mutual responsibilities, but remain flexible to offer support for one another when needed. Both individuals feel that they have worth and value and that they equally contribute to the overall effectiveness of the relationship. Quality couples take time to communicate, share their dreams, goals, hopes, wants, and desires with one another. They challenge and support each other and give one another space and privacy when they sense it is needed. Successful couples never keep track of who has done more or less, who brings in more income or less, because they know relationships are team-oriented, not individualized.

Being healthy begins with you working on you. Do not look to connect on a deep level with another until you are healthy enough to pursue a meaningful relationship. People search every day for signs of happiness that they think will help them make sense of their life. For every person, the search feels and looks completely different. "I'm finally dating someone!" "I got the raise that I deserved." "I just bought the car of my dreams." "My divorce is final." "I just got even." "I'm engaged!" "At last, I had sex." However, without taking care of their physical and mental health, and focusing on the relationships that matter, negative thoughts or feelings will resurface, causing people skepticism about ever achieving true happiness and a sense of fulfillment. There is no shortcut to better health and there is nothing more important.

We cannot read into the future, and thus I understand that I may or may not be present when my daughters begin to date, marry, and have families of their own. I feel confident, however, that I have lived my life in such a way and treated my daughters with such love and respect that they know what healthy looks like, what it sounds like, and what it feels like. I am confident that I have given them a fighting chance for happiness throughout their lives. They are my living legacy to a time that I may never know and to people that I may never meet. The people they are destined to meet have no idea how lucky they are, but I do.

Conclusion

Be Involved

Being involved means identifying someone's needs and reaching out to help them. Compassion draws us closer to someone or something as we place ourselves in their position (or condition) and look at life as they live it. It is often hardest for us to have compassion for those we know best, because we believe they should know better. Why is that? Is it because we have shared our knowledge and expect changes? I believe the answer is "YES!" We expect more from them—and from ourselves. Because you have read this book, I now expect more from you.

I have authored this book because others are in need and I want to reach out and help. A responsibility comes with reading this book and that is you are now required to live a more valuable life and pass on what you have learned to others. It requires you to become more involved with the people and relationships in your life. Maybe you will converse with someone who needs words of encouragement, or perhaps a dose of tough love or to hear your message of concern. Maybe you will listen carefully and intently to someone who needs to be heard and hasn't had an objective and willing audience for some time. Maybe you will hesitate at a door and hold it open for someone you don't even know, or yield your parking spot to another because it is the right thing to do. Maybe you will give a copy of this book to a friend or loved one and discuss topics with them. The scenarios are endless and unpredictable, but knowledge is useless until it is shared, and love is only a concept until it is given away. Help me help others turn meaningful relationships into a reality. Let's touch and change lives. Help turn despair into hope and encourage people to get busy living—the only way to make their relationships truly matter.

Your relationship I.Q. has been raised. You may still make mistakes when it comes to the relationships in your life, but these mistakes will be incidental, made due to haste or choice, because you now have the knowledge and ability to make sound decisions even when faced with tough situations and choices. You now know how to be more courageous. You know how to measure your own value and the value of having others in your life. You know what it means to be healthy and how to help others achieve a similar lifestyle.

We all live through periods of time where we doubt ourselves and wonder if we are actually making a difference. We wonder whether or not we are living up to our potential and affecting other people's lives as we could and should. Do we appreciate the people in our lives and do they appreciate us? Do we matter? When this happens, you need to ask yourself a few important questions:

- Am I happy and satisfied? Why or why not?
- Am I using my God-given gifts and talents?
- Do I have a relationship with God? Do I want one?
- Am I better off because certain people are in my life, and are others better off because I am in theirs?
- Am I making a difference and fulfilling my purpose?
- Do my job and career offer me the satisfaction and flexibility to do the things in my life that I want and need to do?
- Am I taking care of my family and upholding my responsibilities?

The answers, although helpful and somewhat

clarifying, are not as important as the journey it took to reach them. For as you process each question, you process the pattern and status of your life. You have now read this book through once. I encourage you to read it again, only this time use a highlighter to accent those areas of your life that need attention. Identify those areas where you can make a difference in your own life and in another person's life and begin making those changes today. Time is precious and it is in perpetual motion. With every moment you hesitate, you allow time to add separation between what could be, what should be, and what is.

My hope is that you will awaken every day and focus on your physical and mental health and on the relationships that are important to you. To do so requires being as courageous, valuable, respectful, forgiving, passionate, committed, spiritual, trustworthy, healthy, and involved as possible. When this attitude becomes a part of your everyday routine and lifestyle, you will be able to look yourself in the mirror and say, "I lived today with the heart of a champion. I made today matter!" That is the best you can do within your limitation of being human.

Good luck on your journey.

References for Quotes and Information

Page XII. "It is either time to get busy living or get busy dying." Actor Timothy Robbins portraying Andy Dufresne in the movie *The Shawshank Redemption*, 1994, Castle Rock Entertainment and Columbia Pictures Corporation.

Page 1 and Page 9. "A brave man is no different than an ordinary man, he is just braver for five minutes longer." Ralph Waldo Emerson.

Page 15. Curtis Zimmerman quote: "There is no guarantee that your personal September 11th…" taken from a live performance delivered on February 23, 2003, at the MGCA Conference, Chicago, IL, Hyatt Regency O'Hare Airport.

Page 17. Oscar Wilde quote. "A man who knows the price of everything knows the value of nothing."

Page 15. Movie reference, *It's A Wonderful Life*, 1946, Liberty Films. Reference to actor James "Jimmy" Stewart.

Page 28. Curtis Zimmerman quote: "The difference between a dream and a goal…" taken from a live performance delivered on February 23, 2003, at the MGCA Conference, Chicago, IL, Hyatt Regency O'Hare Airport.

Page 33. "You won't find the right person until you become the right person." *The Myth of Romance: Marriage Choices That Last a Lifetime*, Dennis McCallum and Gary DeLashmutt, page 36. Bethany House Publishers, Minneapolis, MN, 1996.

Page 42. "Being mindful…" Alarie Tennille

Page 54. "A blocked goal." Dr. Neil T. Anderson, *Victory Over The Darkness*: *Realizing The Power of Your Identity In Christ*, pp. 126-127. Regal Books, 1990.

Page 56. "Giving up the right to hurt others who have previously hurt you." Dr. Neil T. Anderson, *Victory Over The Darkness: Realizing The Power of Your Identity In Christ*, pp. 201-203. Regal Books, 1990.

Page 58. Movie reference, *What Women Want!* Paramount Pictures, actor Mel Gibson, 2000.

Page 62. "All men die. Some men never live." Actor Mel Gibson portraying William Wallace in the movie *Braveheart*. Paramount Pictures, 1995.

Page 70. "No hunger is so severe that it justifies throwing away God's will to satisfy it." *The Myth of Romance: Marriage Choices That Last a Lifetime*, Dennis McCallum and Gary DeLashmutt, page 16. Bethany House Publishers, Minneapolis, MN 1996.

Page 80. Quote by Darline Clemens. "Passion is about life..." Phone interview conducted on January 6, 2003, Defiance, OH.

Page 85. John Wooden quote taken from live appearance/speech held at Malone College, Canton, OH October, 1977.

Page 91. "About 50% of first time marriages..." The National Center for Health Statistics Report. Bramlett, Matthew and William Mosher. "First marriage dissolution, divorce and remarriage: United States," Advance Data From Vital Health Statistics; No. 323, Hyattsville, MD: National Center for Health Statistics: 2 1.

Page 99. Miriam Hamilton Keare, reprinted in Ann Landers' column, C/O The Canton Repository, Canton, OH. Ann Landers, PO Box 11562, Chicago, IL, 60611.

Page 126. "25 percent of wives and 44 percent of husbands have had extramarital attachments." Shirley P. Glass, Ph. D from interview in The USA Today, p. 12D Wednesday, October 2, 2002. Information is from her book, *NOT "Just Friends": Protect Your Relationship from Infidelity and Heal the Trauma of Betrayal* (The Free Press; January 13, 2003).

Page 127. "It is a lot easier to stay out of trouble than to get out of trouble." Kathleen N. VanHorn. *Indiana Gazette* Mother's Day Quote Contest Winner, November 6, 2001.

Page 141. "When you exercise..." Interview of personal trainer and health club owner Grey Freudenberg, SteelBodies Health and Fitness Club, November 22, 2002, Cincinnati, OH.

MAKING RELATIONSHIPS MATTER

VIDEO SERIES

The Dating Doctor
David D. Coleman

Now available from **www.datingdoctor.com**

Video 1: Building Blocks to Better Relationships

Video 2: Finding the Right Mate

Video 3: Post Break-Up Dating

Video 4: Roadblocks to Trust

Video 5: Enhancing Your Current Relationship

Video 6: Healthy Choices for a Modern World

Video 7: Roadblocks to Intimacy and Commitment

Video 8: Making Our Children's Relationships Matter